THE
ENDURING
PARADOX

THE
ENDURING
PARADOX

EXPLORATORY ESSAYS IN MESSIANIC JUDAISM

General Editor

Dr. John Fischer

Messianic Jewish Publishers
a division of
Messianic Jewish Communications
Baltimore, Maryland

05 04 03 02 01 00   6 5 4 3 2 1

ISBN 1-880226-90-1
Library of Congress classification number 00-133470

Lederer/Messianic Jewish Publishers
a division of
Messianic Jewish Communications
6204 Park Heights Avenue
Baltimore, Maryland 21215
(410) 358-6471

Distributed by
Messianic Jewish Resources International
Individual order line: (800) 410-7367
Trade order line: (800) 773-MJRI (6574)
E-mail: lederer@messianicjewish.net
Website: www.messianicjewish.net

This volume is dedicated to my parents, George and Marianne Fischer; my wife, Patrice; my children, Eve and Seth; and also to my grandparents; all of whom have made it possible for us to be a four generation Messianic Jewish family firmly committed both to Yeshua the Jewish Messiah and to the Jewish traditions.

Contents

Preface

The authors of the essays in this volume are united in their desire to see a firm biblical foundation developed for the benefit of Jewish people who are or may be coming to faith in the Messiah. They also desire to clarify the biblical issues involved in the relationship between Jewish identity, the New Testament, and Israel. They come to their tasks from diverse perspectives. Hopefully this diversity will enable a balanced theological perspective to come into focus. Our hope for soundness and balance comes from our fidelity to the Scriptures.

Our authors unite around these broad tenets:

1. That complete biblical faith must consider the life, death and resurrection of Yeshua (Jesus) the Messiah. He was a Jew as were all of his first followers. Thus it would seem that expressions of the New Testament faith, that are more in keeping with the original cradle of that faith, are valid and appropriate, especially for Jewish people.

2. That the unity of all believers in the Messiah as taught in the New Testament does not call for all individual and cultural differences to be dissolved into one amorphous group. Unity and love in the Messiah are challenges to accept while appreciating diversity.

3. That Israel is God's national people, a chosen nation. Participation in the one people of God through the New Covenant does not and should not cause Jewish people to lose their identity as part of Israel. Thus we look warily at the assimilation of Jewish believers into a gentile Christianity wherein this identity is often lost. Such loss of Jewish identity is detrimental to evangelism among Jewish people and is contrary to God's desire for Israel's salvation. Moreover, it is not God's will that the Jewish people disappear.

We are agreed that a theological foundation for Messianic Judaism is a necessity. Issues need to be explored; many of these explorations will challenge traditional interpretations. Yet, we will only succeed if we submit to the light of the Scriptures.

WHY MESSIANIC JUDAISM?

John Fischer

In order to understand what is happening among Jewish people today and how God is working in our world, our present situation needs to be seen against the backdrop of history. The last century saw two major world wars, energy and food shortages, environmental pollution, political corruption, increased crime, moral decay, international terrorism, and world tensions. These years have made the statement of Sir Winston Churchill seem more and more prophetic: "This generation may well live to see the end of civilization as we now know it."

From the Jewish perspective, beginning with 1967, the years have produced some alarming events and trends as well: several wars in the Middle East, the oil crisis, increased Arab terrorism, the threat against Israel's national existence, Zionism equated with racism in the United Nations, oppression and persecution of Jewish minorities around the world, and a rise of anti-Semitism, even in the U.S. The situation is as Dag Hammarskjold, former U.N. secretary-general, once put it: "I see no hope for a permanent world peace. We've tried hard and failed miserably. Without a spiritual renewal on a worldwide basis, we're doomed."

Yet, despite the discouraging outlook, we can trace God's hand at work in our world, and we can see it quite clearly in relation to the Jewish people. Many Jewish people have expressed a growing spiritual hunger, a searching for God. Dr. Velvel Greene, a Jewish scientist, reflected this tendency: "The Jewish nature and soul needs to know God; it must be told about God. Our souls are looking for God and are trying to know God, and no one has told them."

In addition, the drastic nature of our times has caused some Jewish people to hope for a supernatural solution. One rabbi expressed it this way: "History is rushing to a close. God must intervene as He did in the time of Moses. This is the time when Messiah will come. He might even come tomorrow."

Longings and hopes such as these have become intertwined with a desire for a more personal experience of God and a search for answers to the questions life poses. One rabbi described this phenomenon well, perhaps sarcastically, but appropriately:

> We are living in an age where people want to touch, approach and feel God. Judaism has always been very abstract . . . (It) raises more questions than it answers. The Jesus movement has all the answers.[1]

As a result, a growing number of Jews have accepted Yeshua as Messiah. This trend has alarmed many rabbis, some of whom have estimated that 2,000–3,000 Jewish people make this decision each year.

Still another aspect of the positive response is the growing Jewish interest in Jesus. Evidence of this appears in a number of ways. Israeli public schools have taught the Old Testament for years. Several years ago the school system launched a program to teach the gospels and the life of Jesus to junior high students. Another example comes from academic circles. Important Jewish scholars such as David Flusser and Pinchas Lapide have spoken and written very positively about Jesus. For example: "We are proud of our Einsteins, Heinrich Heines and Sigmund Freuds; we ought to be much prouder of Jesus."[2]

Yet, poles apart from this is another response. It views evangelism as a threat to Jewish survival, as an attempt to wipe out Judaism. For example, Rabbi Stanley Rubinowitz stated that "[Evangelism] promotes a stifling, suppressive climate, intrudes on the privacy of Jews, plans their quick liquidation and extinction, and shelters . . . anti-Semitism" (quoted by Susan Perlman in "The Furor over Jewish evangelism," *Eternity*, April 1973, p. 22).

Or, to put it more bluntly, "This mission business is just like murder. We might as well lose one to Hitler as to the Christians." Beyond this, many Jews perceive Christianity as permeated with anti-Jewish sentiment, which makes it virtually impossible for them to consider Christianity as a serious option.

Psychologically, Christianity is too intimately involved in Jewish minds with the guilt of the Holocaust for Jews to be able to speak or listen freely to it; and the silence of organized Christianity during the Six Day War only increased those emotional barriers.[3]

Why is there such confusion about Christianity? History provides more answers.

The Reasons for the Antagonism

A number of occurrences emphasizing the "aloneness" and "distinctiveness" of the Jewish people triggered this response. These occurrences justified the Jews' right to consider themselves especially threatened and, therefore, worthy of all efforts to insure their survival.

Certain groups have responded antagonistically to Israel as a matter of course. Jewish people over the years fought side by side with many of these groups for the same causes. Since the Six Day War in 1967 many activists have shown increasingly anti-Israel, pro-Arab attitudes. They denounce Israel as imperialistic, militaristic and racist. This conflicts with the Jewish people's love for Israel. So, many Jews have felt that their former friends have turned on them and left them alone in a time of crisis. Only Jews have shown any concern for Jewish problems.

Also, many ethnic groups in the United States have emphasized self-identity. Irish-American, Polish-American and Italian-Americans have become labels of pride and distinction. This has helped to legitimize Jewish self-identity and active support of Jewish interests.

The "rediscovery" of the Holocaust probably contributed most to the Jewish people's self-awareness. For many, the Holocaust had become a fading memory. Jewish young people remained oblivious to the events that had brutally exterminated two-thirds of Europe's Jewish population. The whole horror of the Holocaust was revived when Arab leaders promised to push the Israelis into the sea. This raised the possibility of genocide once again. The world had stood by once before while the Nazis liquidated Jews. The world's response to the Middle East wars indicated that things had not changed much.

For two long weeks in May 1967, the worldwide
Jewish community perceived the specter of a second Jewish Holocaust in a single generation. For
two weeks, it listened to the same words emanating
from Cairo and Damascus which had once ema-
nated from Berlin. For two weeks, it longed for
Christian words of apprehension and concern. But,
whereas some such words came from secular
sources, from the churches there was little but silence. Once again, Jews were alone.[4]

The two wars, as well as the oil crisis and repeated anti-Israel U.N.
resolutions, not only demonstrated the isolation of the Jewish
people, but other nations' (beside Arab nations') animosity toward
them as well. The Yom Kippur War provided another excellent example. Very few nations expressed any alarm when the combined
Arab armies attacked Israel on the most holy day of the Jewish year.
They made no outcry when Arab armies overran Israeli defenses
and threatened to crush Israel. Even the United States delayed its
aid. The first sign of alarm occurred only when the battle's tide
changed and the Israeli army began advancing toward Cairo and
Damascus. Not until then did any nation attempt to stop the war.
The world cared little for Jewish lives. However, they did show
concern for the availability of Arab oil.

Thus, a number of events have highlighted the Jewish people's
isolation. Also, they reinforced the meaning and lessons of the Holocaust: any trust in Gentiles must be cautious and tentative, at
best; there is no certainty that what happened in Nazi Germany will
not be repeated. As a result, Jewish survival achieved a deep, new
significance. Jews concluded that survival had become God's command for the Jewish people, and they must make every effort to
ensure it. Jews insisted on being and remaining Jewish, and repeated a familiar statement more frequently: "I was born a Jew, and
I'll die a Jew."

This attitude resulted in Jewish people strenuously opposing
anything that even appeared to threaten their survival and identity.

What the victory (1967) did for us and perhaps for
most American Jews, was to reinforce a thousand-
fold a new determination to resist . . . To resist any

who would in any way and to any degree and for
any reason whatsoever attempt to do us any harm,
any who would diminish us or destroy us, any who
would challenge our right and our duty to look after ourselves and our families, any who would deny
us the right to pursue our own interests or frustrate
us in our duty to do so.[5]

Correspondingly, concerned Jews intensified the attack on assimilation and the factors contributing to it. One writer described the
new attitudes as "the commanding voice of Auschwitz," one of the
most notorious of Hitler's death camps, a frequent symbol of the
entire Holocaust.

Jews are forbidden to grant posthumous victories
to Hitler. They are commanded to survive as Jews,
lest the Jewish people perish. They are commanded
to remember the victims of Auschwitz, lest their
memory perish. They are forbidden to despair of
man and his world, and to escape in either cynicism
or otherworldliness, lest they cooperate in the de-
livering of the world over to the forces of
Auschwitz. Finally, they are forbidden to despair of
the God of Israel, lest Judaism perish. A secular Jew
cannot make himself believe by a mere act of the
will, nor can he be commanded to do so; yet, he
can perform the commandment of Auschwitz, and
a religious Jew who has stayed with his God may be
forced into new, possibly revolutionary, relationships with Him.

One possibility, however, is wholly unthinkable. A Jew may not respond to Hitler's attempt to
destroy Judaism by himself cooperating in its destruction. In ancient times, the unthinkable Jewish
sin was idolatry. Today, it is to respond to Hitler by
doing his work.[6]

In the light of history, a Jewish person simply cannot consider as a
viable option anything which even remotely contributes to
Judaism's breakdown.

Another realm of history out of which Jewish antagonism to the gospel arises goes back 1600 years. It revolves around the historical relationship between the church and the synagogue, an area which at this point can only be briefly surveyed. Unfortunately, much persecution of Jewish people has taken place in Jesus' name; admittedly, most of it was perpetrated by those not truly his followers. However, there are some significant exceptions.

As far back as the fourth century, John Chrysostom, an important church leader and committed follower of Jesus, wrote of the Jewish people:

> [They are] inveterate murders, destroyers, men possessed by the devil . . . They have surpassed the ferocity of wild beasts, for they murder their offspring and immolate them to the devil . . . The Jewish disease must be guarded against . . . The Christian's duty is to hate the Jews.[7]

Years later, during the Crusades, after the intervening years had intensified these attitudes, various Crusader armies massacred tens of thousands of Jewish people on their marches. For example, at the end of the first Crusade, in 1099, the Crusaders gathered the Jews of Jerusalem into the Great Synagogue and then burned it to the ground with men, women and children inside. The Crusaders marched under the flag of the cross, it should be noted.

The situation worsened during the Inquisition. Forced baptisms, confiscation of property, torture and burning at the stake characterized this period for the Jewish people. It culminated in the sudden expulsion of the entire Jewish population of the Spanish Empire. More than one quarter of a million people were forced from their homes and left to wander and face the elements. The Inquisition, too, was carried out under the banner of the cross.

Although the Reformation eased anti-Jewish attitudes, problems did persist. Luther, after earlier expressing sympathy, charged Jews with being poisoners, ritual murderers and parasites. He went on to say:

> The Jews are brutes, their synagogues are pigsties; they ought to be burned . . . They live by evil and

plunder; they are wicked beasts that ought to be
driven out like mad dogs.[8]

Calvin did little better, calling Jews "profane, bark-
ing dogs, as stupid as cattle, a confounded rabble."[9]

Strong anti-Jewish sentiment has persisted in "Christian" circles
even into the twentieth century, the century marked by the Holocaust. Some might find it repulsive to include the Holocaust as part
of a survey of church-synagogue relations. Yet, since Hitler came
from a "Christian" country, which he then used as the instrument
for his purposes, his program is viewed—by Jews—in connection
with Christianity's relations to Judaism.

Furthermore, Hitler himself wrote in *Mein Kampf*:

> Hence today I believe that I am acting in accor-
> dance with the will of the Almighty Creator. By
> defending myself against the Jew, I am fighting for
> the work of the Lord."[10]

Admittedly, this has been a selective survey, but it is presented
to show the kinds of things Jewish people remember of Judaism's
historical contacts with Christianity. By way of example, a number
of years ago a prominent seminary president visited Israel. While
there, he asked his Israeli guide, "When I use the term 'Christian,'
what comes to your mind?" The guide responded, "The Crusades,
the Inquisition and Nazi Germany." A well-known Jewish rabbi
and author aptly summarized this Jewish attitude:

> Since the tree is to be judged by its fruits, the stan-
> dards and values of this religion and civilization
> have become questionable . . . in view of the
> Christian's performance through the ages, Chris-
> tianity has never been as dead an option for the Jew
> as it is today.[11]

History has certainly contributed to the confusion concerning
Christianity.

The Role of Messianic Judaism

Beginning in the seventies, independently of one another and of any "outside" organization, congregations of Jewish and Gentile believers sprang up in Jewish communities across the United States. The convictions of these congregations are unique. They are convinced that they can believe in Jesus, be thoroughly biblical, and yet authentically Jewish. They affirm Jesus as Messiah, Savior and Lord of the universe. They adhere to the entire Bible as the inspired Word of God and refuse to do anything contrary to its teachings. They feel a kinship and commitment to the entire body of the Messiah. Yet, they express their faith, lifestyle and worship in Jewish forms and in Jewish ways.

Jewish believers—as well as Gentiles who desire to worship in a Jewish context—formed themselves into congregations in Jewish communities, where they express their faith in Jesus and affirm their Jewishness, while being thoroughly biblical. They speak of themselves as Messianic Jews, call Jesus by his given Hebrew name "Yeshua," and visibly demonstrate that a Jew can commit himself to following Yeshua as the Messiah and strengthen—not dilute—his Jewish identity. Messianic congregations or synagogues do not threaten Jewish survival; instead, they enhance it. As such, they are very much in step with the emphasis of the Jewish community on Jewish identity and survival.

While this Messianic Jewish expression is relatively new for our times, it reaches back over 1900 years. In the Sermon on the Mount, Yeshua (Jesus) said he came not to abolish the Law and prophets—the basis of the Jewish way of worship and life—but to fulfill it (Matt. 5:17–19).

The term "abolish" means "to set aside or abrogate," while the term "fulfill"—in the Greek—means "to cram full, bring to full expression, confirm, show forth in its true meaning."[12] And, the two terms, abolish and fulfill, are set in strong contrast to each other. The Apostles understood the intent of Yeshua's words, as their practices demonstrated. They continued to worship daily in the Temple (Acts 2:46; 3:1). They, including Paul, celebrated the Jewish holidays (Acts 20:5–6, 16; 27:9). They observed the customs and traditions (Acts 21:20–26). For example, Paul, speaking in his own defense, claimed that he had done nothing wrong against Jewish law, Temple practice, or religious tradition (Acts

25:8; 28:17). In fact, he urged the first century Messianic Jews to maintain their Jewish lifestyles (Acts 21:20–26; 1 Cor. 7:18).

Ancient historians provide further confirmation. Josephus records the martyrdom of James, Yeshua's brother, as well as his piety and faithfulness to the Jewish traditions. When James was killed at the instigation of the high priest, the Pharisees—out of respect for his piety and consistency as a Jew—complained to the Roman government so forcibly that Rome had the high priest deposed![13] Irenaeus, who stood in a direct line to the Apostles, wrote: "But they themselves . . . continued in the ancient observances . . . thus did the apostles . . . scrupulously act according to the dispensation of the Mosaic law."[14]

The modern Messianic Jews attempt to imitate the way their ancient forebears lived, worshipped and communicated as part of the Jewish community. The results have been exciting.

Gentiles who have become part of the congregations—as well as those who visit—have been enthusiastic about discovering the roots of their faith. They have been enriched by seeing the significance of many biblical practices and by learning how Jewish practices beautifully picture the life and relationship with God that Yeshua provides. They have also learned how an understanding of Jewish backgrounds assists in better understanding both testaments of the Bible. And, those who have desired it have become fully integrated into these Messianic congregations.

A prominent rabbi's observation summarizes another consequence of Messianic Judaism: "In the past, Jews who have [become believers in Jesus] were largely on the periphery of Jewish life. A large percentage were cranks and crackpots. Now it is quite different in this very significant respect."[15]

The mainstream of the Jewish community has been much more favorable to hearing about the Messiah because of these congregations. When they visit, they observe things recognizable as authentically Jewish and yet, perceive the difference that faith in Yeshua provides. In fact, an increasingly more significant proportion of Jewish people have been impacted by the Messianic synagogues. Jewish community agencies have estimated that there are some 350,000 Messianic Jews in the United States.[16] As one Jewish newspaper noted, more Jewish people have accepted Yeshua as Messiah in the last 20 years than in the past 20 centuries.[17]

The Messianic synagogues have attracted Jewish people of all ages who come from different religious backgrounds, from orthodox to atheistic. As a result, the Jewish community has been afforded a less-threatening opportunity and environment in which to investigate the claims of Yeshua. One recent visitor expressed it well: "Now I can definitely see that you can be Jewish and believe in Jesus."

These congregations, and the Messianic Jewish movement of which they are a part, have raised some biblical and theological issues, in addition to providing fresh and unique insights into the Scriptures and into biblical faith.

The following articles are grouped around three issues—Messianic Jewish Theology, Messianic Jews and Israel, and Practical Matters for Messianic Jews and non-Jews. It is to these issues that we now turn.

1. Stanley Rubinowitz, quoted in "The Furor Over Jewish Evangelism," by Susan Perlman, *Eternity*, April 1973, p. 22.

2. Pinchas Lapide, *New York Times*, Feb. 2, 1978. Also see the positive treatment in David Flusser's book, which was recently revised, *Jesus*, Magnes Press, 1997.

3. Eugene Borowitz, *How Can a Jew Speak of Faith Today?* Westminster Press, 1969, p. 208.

4. Emil Fackenheim, *Quest for Past and Future*, Indiana University Press, 1968, p. 24.

5. Norman Podhoretz, "A Certain Anxiety," *Commentary*, August 1971, p. 6.

6. Emil Fackenheim, "Jewish Faith and the Holocaust," *Commentary*, August 1968.

7. *Homilies Against the Jews*, 1:4–6; 4; 5.

8. *Concerning the Jews and Their Lies*.

9. *Corpus Reformatorum*, see 40:605; 50:307; et. al.

10. Lucy Dawidowitz, *The War Against the Jews*, pp. 219–20.

11. Eliezer Berkovits, *Faith After the Holocaust*, KTAV, 1973, p. 24.

12. A Greek-English Lexicon of the New Testament and Other Early Christian Literature, ed. W.F. Arndt and F.W. Gingrich, University of Chicago Press, 1967.

13. *Antiquities*, XX.9.1.

14. *Against Heresies*, 3.23.15.

15. Harry Siegman, quoted in "Everyone's Talking About Those Jewish Christians," by Hefley, *Moody Monthly*, May 1973, p. 27.

16. Jewish Community Relations Council of New York Survey, cited in *Petah Tikvah*, October–December, 1989.

17. *The Jewish Press of Pinellas County*, June 2, 1989, p. 2.

Section I

MESSIANIC JEWISH THEOLOGY

MESSIANIC PROPHECIES IN THE OLD TESTAMENT

Walter C. Kaiser, Jr.

There are some 456 Old Testament passages which refer to the Messiah or Messianic times, attested in 558 separate quotations from the Rabbinic writings.[1] While it may be freely conceded that some of these references are questionable due to the subjective methodology and "spiritualizing" tendencies in Rabbinic interpretation, nevertheless, the statistics alone remain as an eloquent testimony to both the plethora of available Old Testament texts and the strong Jewish consciousness that the hope of salvation and the glory of God's people was indeed connected with the prospect of a coming ideal king who would rule the world.

The Nature of Messianic Prophecies

Before actually considering a selection of these passages, inquiry must first be made into the nature and character of these Messianic passages. By what term or terms are we to refer to this doctrine? Is the doctrine a result of scattered predictions which later made sense when Christ appeared or is there an eternal plan which knowingly was unfolded before the eyes of Israel and all the world? How many peoples and how much material did the doctrine of Messiah embrace as it grew during Old Testament days? These questions must be addressed first before we turn to the content itself.

Messiah or Servant?

What was this coming Redeemer-King most frequently called? Almost universally, he is referred to today as the Messiah. Now this is somewhat strange, since if one were to judge simply on the frequency of the terms used, he would have selected the biblical term "Servant of the Lord." This term is the most prominent term, appearing in Isa. 40–66 thirty-one times in connection with the coming Redeemer-King. Furthermore, these passages were cited more often by the New Testament writers than any others, except for those promises which were given to Abraham and David.

But the designation of "Servant" apparently was too often connected solely with the aspect of suffering and the death of the coming person, thus, the more regal term won out.

To be sure, "Messiah" does appear some thirty-nine times in the Old Testament, but the term was used to designate the "anointed" High Priest four times (Lev. 4:3, 5, 16; 6:22), twice of the patriarchs (Ps. 105:15; 1 Chron. 16:22), and once of Cyrus (Isa. 45:1). In the majority of the passages, which appear in the books of Samuel and Psalms, it has reference to one of the "anointed" Israelite kings: Saul, David, Solomon. This leaves only nine passages to refer exclusively to a coming person, but all nine are hotly contested. But surely Ps. 2:2 and Dan. 9:25, 26 clearly depict a Messiah who was yet to come. Perhaps 1 Sam. 2:20 and 2:35 could be added to this list.[2]

Regardless of the decision made on the term itself, the fact is clear: numerous texts refer to a coming king who will redeem men from their sin and who will possess an everlasting kingdom to which the nations of the earth must one day yield either willingly or unwillingly.

Prediction or Promise

While it may not seem to make much difference whether we think of the Old Testament words about Messiah's person and work as predictions or a promise, there is a vast difference for the Biblical authors. A prediction is a foretelling or a prognostication. It concentrates the hearer's or reader's attention only on two things: the word spoken before the event and the fulfilling event itself. Certainly, this is proper and legitimate, for it does magnify the greatness of God's word and the accuracy of his accomplishing that ancient word; however, it fails to capture precisely that aspect which thrilled the Old Testament writers and saints.

Promise, on the other hand, embraces, as Willis J. Beecher remarked:

> . . . The means employed for that purpose. The promise and the means and the result are all in mind at once. . . . If the promise involved a series of results, we might connect any one of the results with the foretelling clause as a fulfilled prediction. . . . But if we permanently confined our thought to these items in the fulfilled promise, we should be led to an inadequate and very likely a false idea of the promise and its fulfillment. To understand the predictive element aright we must see it in the light of the other elements. Every fulfilled promise is a fulfilled prediction; but it is exceedingly important to look at it as a promise and not as mere prediction.[3]

Since so much if not all of Old Testament prophecy falls into the class of a series of predictions with many of them having a series of results, the necessity for regarding these prophecies as promises rather than merely as predictions becomes obvious.

Separate or Cumulative?

Of even greater importance is the matter of the interrelation of these prophecies. Even granting that some may be in a series, are the series interrelated? Or are we dealing with disconnected and heterogeneous predictions randomly announced in the Word of God?

The marvel of prophecy is neither in an alleged separation of the prophetic word from history and geography nor in an unproven assumption that prediction is the main feature in prophecy. Rather, the amazing thing about Old Testament predictions concerning Messiah and his work is that they all make up one continuous plan of God. There is unity here, not diverse and scattered predictions. Each prediction is interfitted into the continuous promise of God which was first announced to pre-patriarchal peoples, enlarged and continuously supplemented from the patriarchs down to the post-exilic era of Haggai, Zechariah, and Malachi. But it remained God's single, cumulative promise.

Precisely the reverse emphasis was the weakness of some of the great apologetic works on prophecy in the past. Indeed, they did correctly show how literally hundreds of predictions have come true in Messiah, but they either exhausted the reader and themselves in trying to show that the scattered Old Testament texts did indeed predict these seemingly unrelated facts and they were therefore entitled to use that text; or they often just assumed that the connection between the Old Testament word and the accomplished events was understood by all so that any whimsical impressions left by the selection of the precise Old Testament words was not worth considering in light of such vastly greater gains made in the interest of apologetics. But all along, the unity and cumulative force of the prophecies went begging for lack of interpreters and careful readers. The very repetition of previous prophecies in the later ones should have pointed to the fact that God's revelation was building on what had been previously announced.

Temporal or Eternal?

The duration of this continuous series of announcements in the single, ancient, but renewing promise of God must also be part of our concern when we speak of the character and nature of Messianic prophecy. Too often, reference is made to the fulfillment of separate prophecies as if they were the final enactment of all that God had intended. What should have been said instead was that there was a climacteric fulfillment in the first advent of Christ, i.e. an important change had been reached in the ongoing development of the promise. However, this was no final fulfillment, nor is any other event God's final fulfillment, for the promise is an everlasting promise enduring to all of eternity.

The time-range of the Messianic prophecies is staggering. It begins in Eden with a word about a "seed" that would remedy the Fall and continues on into the everlasting kingdom of God where Christ reigns as sovereign Lord over the nations in the new heavens and the new earth. The sweep is breathtaking, but it also has a unitized character. Wherever the word of promise is met in the Old Testament, it also participates in that "eternal covenant" (e.g. Heb. 13:20) which made the Word so dependable and certain (Gal. 3:15–18; Rom. 11:29; Heb. 6:13, 17–18).

Cosmopolitan or National?

All of this brings up a delicate point in Jewish and Christian interpretation. If the promise made with Abraham on through to David, and those who followed, is eternal (Gen. 17:7, 13, 19; 2 Sam. 23:5; Ps. 89:29; Isa. 55:3), then what must be done with the persistent inclusions about Israel's national career and her geographical holdings?

Some Jewish and nationalistic scholars conclude that since Israel's geographical and political career is included so obviously in the center of the promise, that is all that the promise means. It was a prophetic hope expressing the demographic and political aspirations of the nation Israel; consequently all other applications to the Church or especially to Jesus Christ are false and inapplicable. This conclusion fails to take the Old Testament itself seriously, much less the historical realities.

On the other hand, an overwhelming number of Christian interpreters err in the same manner, only to the opposite side of the promise. They deny that the promise has anything left in it for national Israel, unless it be just incidentally, now that the Christian era has arrived.

Willis J. Beecher of the Old Princeton faculty said it best when he commented:

> . . . If the Christian interpreter persists in excluding the ethnical Israel from his conception of the fulfillment, or in regarding Israel's part in the matter as merely preparatory and not eternal, then he comes into conflict with the plain witness of both Testaments [and we might now add "with history as well"]. . . . Rightly interpreted, the biblical statements include in the fulfillment both Israel the race, with whom the covenant is eternal, and also the personal Christ and his mission, with the whole spiritual Israel of the redeemed in all ages. The New Testament teaches this as Christian doctrine, for

leading men to repentance and for edification, and
the Old Testament teaches it as messianic doctrine, for leading men to repentance and for edification. . . . The exclusive Jewish interpretation
and the exclusive Christian interpretation are
equally wrong. Each is correct in what it affirms,
and incorrect in what it denies.[4]

The promise, then, was national *and* cosmopolitan. Israel will yet
receive what God's eternal covenant had unconditionally promised: a land, nationhood, king, worship and riches. But so will the
nations of the earth be blessed in Abraham's seed. Indeed all the
ends of the earth shall turn to the Lord (Ps. 2:7, 8) and princes
shall come from Egypt and Ethiopia and sing unto God (Ps. 68:31,
32). So agreed Isaiah (49:12, 22; 60:3, 5, 11; 61:6; 62:2; 66:19)
and all the prophets. Was not the Jerusalem Council convened to
answer this very question? And did they not appeal successfully to
the satisfaction of the Jews present there to Amos 9:11–12? And if
any doubt remains concerning the Jew, hasn't Paul spoken defini-
tively in Rom. 11?

Therefore we conclude that the Messianic doctrine is located in
God's single unified plan, called his promise, which is eternal in its
fulfillment, with climacteric plateaus reached in its historical ac-
complishments. Finally, it is cumulative in its build-up, but national and truly cosmopolitan in its outreach to all nations, tribes
and peoples in all historical times.

The Unfolding Doctrine of Messiah

E. Jenni summarized the situation best when he observed that:

. . . The Old Testament Messiah . . . has no real
counterpart in the ancient Near Eastern milieu. Its
source must, therefore, be sought within the Old
Testament faith. To be sure, many of the concepts
which are a part of the picture of Messiah are also to
be found in the intellectual world of the
Babylonians, the Egyptians, and other cultures of
the Near East. But in these cases, they lack the spe-

cifically Israelite projection toward the final goal of history.[5]

It is to that testament, then, that we turn to receive the word of promise, and some of its results in history tip to the first advent.

The Roots of the Promise

At least two passages constitute the tap roots of the promise in the pre-patriarchal era. The first was given to Adam and Eve in Gen. 3:15 and the other was given to Shem in Gen. 9:26–27.

In the former passage, the earliest beginnings of the Messiah can be ever so faintly observed. But make no mistake about it; the presence of a promise which began a long series of amplifications which at once formed a doctrine of salvation, a direction for the universal history of mankind, and a cryptic statement about the outcome of the whole process is as certain as words can be.

A divinely imposed hostility ("I will cause") between personalities ("enmity" is a word always used between individuals, never involving the lower creation) is announced in Gen. 3:15. The contest will at first be between (1) Satan and (2) Eve; then between (3) Satan's "seed" and (4) Eve's "seed." The collective or corporate nature of the word "seed" is most important for understanding any Messianic doctrine, for it is the first of many to come. It involves the total group meant (either all the physical or spiritual descendants) and then it comes to its fullest realization in its representative head who epitomizes the whole group. Thus, the seed of Satan is, no doubt, all his spiritual descendants who are to live subsequently on the earth and who will one day be singularly represented and epitomized in the Antichrist who is to come according to later revelation. But the seed of Eve are all her future spiritual descendants who will also be effectively represented in the One, himself the "Seed" too, viz., Jesus Christ.[6] (This is also Paul's insight into Moses' meaning, cf. Gal. 3:16, 29).

The real surprise, however, is not the divinely implanted hostility between 1 vs 2 or 3 vs 4; it is that a 4a, a male descendant of Eve's seed, would be victoriously matched in a battle with (1) "Satan." He would mortally crush Satan—which victory Paul later added would be shared by all the seed of Eve (Rom. 16:20).

How this victory would be actualized and what the wounding of this man's heel meant had to await later unfolding revelation.

In the meantime, the circle of possible origins for this deliverer for man's desperate need is given in Gen. 9:26–27. With tantalizing brevity, the promise is simply, "Blessed be the LORD, the God of Shem; he shall dwell in the tents of Shem."

To be sure, the subject of "he shall dwell" is extremely difficult to ascertain. Charles Briggs strenuously argued that it was the same as the subject of the preceding clause and therefore this dwelling was an open prediction that God would one day come and "tabernacle" among the Semitic peoples.[7] This suggestion must not be dismissed as quickly as it has been customarily treated. However, even if the subject is, as most argue, Japhet, then the text still identifies Shem as the fountain head of all divine blessing. Non-Semitic peoples, like Japhet, will need to find their spiritual provision from the "Shemites."

The Promise to Abraham

In Abraham's day the doctrine of Messiah took a giant step forward. God met with one of Shem's descendants and narrowed the circle from which the divine blessing should emanate even further.

The word to Abraham, Isaac and Jacob centered on a promised heir (Gen. 12:3, 7; 13:14–16; 15:4–5, 13, 18; 16:10; 17:2, 7, 9, 19; 21:12; 22:17; 26:24; 27:28, 29; 28:14). The promise of a "seed" brought to the patriarch's mind, no doubt, the ancient word given to Adam and Eve about a "seed," indeed a coming "heir" who would crush Satan's head. Thus, a "seed" is developing which at once includes all believers, but which also simultaneously has its ultimate sights set on a single heir par excellence: The One who would represent the many. When Abraham was asked to sacrifice Isaac on Mt. Moriah (Gen. 22), the full meaning of what it meant to have the promise of God's heir came home to the patriarch with full force. God alone was capable of maintaining his promise, and, as if to underscore the point, God took an oath to confirm this work. He also was able to provide a substitute for bound Isaac. Is it any wonder, then, that Jesus insisted on the fact that "Abraham rejoiced to see my day, he saw it and was glad"?

Meanwhile, a series of fresh births of sons (like Isaac and Jacob), which stood in a direct line with this coming person, testified to the reality of the promise and they themselves each revealed part of the accomplishment in their own historical times. Along with promising an heir, the LORD included an inheritance of the land of Canaan as a gift to the patriarchs and their descendants forever (Gen. 12:1, 7; 13:15, 17; 15:7, 18; 17:8; 24:7; 26:2, 23; 28:13; 49:8–12). Thereby, the doctrine of Messiah was tied in directly with an earthly philosophy of history. His kingdom would not only be spiritually located in the hearts of his men, but it would also be located in our planet and in our history as well. He would, appropriately, complete history as he had begun it with his people Israel in their land. Present-day Christians must not jettison this provision in the Messianic doctrine for supposed theological or hermeneutical reasons when all along it is actually the result of "our Western dualism, docetism and spiritualism."[8]

A third and climactic provision found in that same Abrahamic promise was the gift of a heritage that in the patriarch's seed "the nations of the earth shall be blessed" (Gen. 12:3; 18:18; 26:4; 28:14). So excellent was this provision that it is uniformly called the "gospel" (e.g. Gal. 3:8). All nations, peoples and tribes would be blessed [not "bless themselves"],[9] i.e., hear about: God's heir/ Messiah, God's plan and philosophy of history wherein the nation Israel became God's timepiece, and a gospel rich enough to save all who would believe.

Thus God chose Abram from the line of Shem and made his seed the center of the promise for the future redemption of the entire world. As if to anticipate the royal predictions of Jacob (Gen. 49:8–10) and Balaam (Num. 24:17) which ultimately rested in David's house (2 Sam. 7), God promised to make Abram and Sarai ancestors of kings (Gen. 17:6; cf. 35:11).

Jacob, in his blessing, had prophetically given to his fourth son, Judah, the scepter of kingship which was to be his "until he comes to whom it belongs" (cf. "Shiloh" and Ezek. 21:27). That one was none other than Messiah, just as the angel announced in Luke 1:32–33. Similarly, Balaam also saw royalty, and as a star and a scepter coming out of Israel. Messiah now was known to be not only from the "seed" of Eve, Shem and Abraham; but more specifically, he was to be a reigning son from Judah's tribe.

The Everlasting Priesthood

Before Scripture spells out in detail all that this coming ruler would be like, it adds two other offices to his kingship: priest and prophet. Both of these promises also appear to be generic and corporate in nature; that is, they predict a series of men holding these offices, while also envisioning a culminating personage as a climacteric fulfillment.

Even though all Israel has been characterized as a "kingdom of priests" before the LORD (Exod. 19:5–6) and had declined the offer because of God's awesome holiness, in Num. 25:12–13, Phinehas's righteous act led God to promise that henceforth he and his "seed" after him would receive a covenant of an "everlasting priesthood." This prophecy was expanded on the eve of the demise of Eli's house. On that occasion, God said that he would raise up a "faithful priest" and "build him a permanent house and he would walk before his anointed [Messiah] forever" (1 Sam. 2:35).

Delitzsch summarized this aspect precisely when he said:

> The promise (I Sam. 2:35) is primarily realized in all the better Zadokite high priests who stood at the side of the better kings from the house of David. But its ultimate fulfillment is found in the Christ of God, in whom according to Zech. 6:13 the ideal king and priest do not stand side by side but are united.[10]

The only correction needed to Delitzsch's statement is that already 500 years earlier, David had contemplated in Ps. 110:4, 6 this union of a "priest" "after the order of Melchizedek" and a victorious "Lord" who would judge the nations. No doubt, when David received this revelation in Psalm 110, he was having his "quiet time" in Gen. 14 and while contemplating the sweet victory that God had given to his man of promise, Abraham,[11] over the four foreign kings, his mind was filled with the prospect of a future victory when the LORD would one day also say to David's LORD, "sit at my right hand."

The Prophet Like Moses

Likewise, Deut. 18:15, 18 pointed to "a prophet" who would come from among the Jews and be like Moses. While it is technically true that the expression, "I will raise up to you a prophet," is not collective or generic, but denotes only one prophet and no more, all the same the word is used here also in a distributive sense. It appears in a context which speaks of priests, Levites and false prophets as classes. Nor is there any Pentateuchal passage authorizing later prophecy if this is not it. Indeed, all previous Messianic prophecy has been generic as is the prophecy that follows in the next period. Consequently, while focusing on that one prophet who was to come, the context leads us to expect a succession of prophets.

This is exactly how Peter viewed our passage in Acts 3:21, 24, as did Stephen in Acts 7:37. The line of true prophets was consummated in Jesus Christ.

Others distinguished between that great prophet and the Messiah (John 1:19–21; 4:19, 25; 6:14; 7:40–42) while the unity of the two perhaps dawned on others (Matt. 21:9–11).

Already in Deut. 33:5, Moses had been called "king," and in Exod. 34:3–8 he was Israel's first priest, indeed the judge of Aaron's office (Lev. 10:1–20) and the one who passed the high-priesthood on Eleazar (Num. 20:23–29). Thus Scripture provided for the ultimate unification of the Messiah's offices in Moses' functions; there was to be a resemblance of Moses' ministry as priest and king.[12]

The Sure Mercies of David

The future redemption of the race was to come through the seed of the woman, the race of Shem, the promise of Abraham, the ruling scepter and star in Judah, the kingdom of priests in Israel, the priesthood of Phinehas and the prophet like Moses.

But the best of all was now to be disclosed by Nathan the prophet in 2 Sam. 7 (1 Chron. 17). The same promise that had been extended a millennium earlier to Abraham and had continued through his seed in the meantime, is now given another gigantic push forward with the news that God would establish

David's dynasty ("house"), kingdom and throne forever. Furthermore, the duration was not only eternal, but the realm of the kingdom was universal.

In flabbergasted tones, David thanks God in a prayer that divulges the fact that David understood this promise to be a "Charter for all humanity" (2 Sam. 7:19).[13] This accords with the eloquent heights of the Davidic and Solomonic Messianic Psalms such as 2, 45, 72 and 110. Yes, "all kings will fall down before him: all nations shall serve him" (Ps. 72:10).

The prophetic literature sharpens the specifics on the Davidic dynasty ("house"), authority ("throne") and rule or realm ("kingdom"). This future king will be born in David's city of Bethlehem (Mic. 5:2), enjoy a miraculous birth ("sign" of Isa. 7:14), be called "God," the "Everlasting Father" (Isa. 9:6), and have the "Spirit of the LORD" resting upon him (Isa. 11:2). He is to be the "one" good "shepherd" that will rule over Israel (Ezek. 34:23–24) as "king" in accordance with the "everlasting covenant" made previously with Abraham and David, but now in its enlarged form called a "new covenant" (Jer. 31:31ff.) or "covenant of peace" (Ezek. 37:24–28). All this is but a partial list of those "sure mercies" given to David (Isa. 55:3).

The Servant of the LORD

Integrally wound up with these themes of royalty and victory was the theme of suffering Messiah. The principle of ransom or deliverance on the basis of an appointed substitute had already been taught by Moses as an "everlasting statute" in the Passover lamb (Exod. 12:14) and in the two goats of the Day of Atonement (Lev. 16:34). The perpetuity of this principle finds its concrete embodiment in the person of Isaiah's servant of the Lord.

The term "servant" is again a generic or collective term which according to Isaiah's own teaching often meant "Israel," precisely what the "seed" of the earlier promises signified (Isa. 41:8–10; 42:18–19; 43:9–10; 44:1–3, 21; 45:4; 48:20; 49:3; Jer. 30:10; 46:27, 28; Ezek. 28:25; and the plural word, "servants," all coming after Isa. 53; viz, 54:17; 56:6; 63:17; 65:8–9, 13, 14–15; and 66:14). Notice, however, this is not merely ethnic Israel; it is Israel as possessor of the promise given to Abraham and David—national Israel and spiritual Israel.[14]

But then this servant also is to be distinguished from national Israel in that he is an individual who has a mission to Israel (Isa. 42:1–7; 49:1–9; 50:4–10; 52:13–53:12; Jer. 33:21; Ezek. 34:23, 24; 37:24, 25; Hag. 2:23; Zech 3:8). The term is technical, but clear. Can anyone doubt that his "Servant" is the same as the Kingly Messiah when they share attributes (e.g. "my Spirit is on him"; Isa. 42:1, cf. Isa. 11:2) and the same mission (e.g. "a light to the Gentiles"; Isa. 42:6; 49:6; cf. Isa. 9:2)?

However, let there be no mistake. God's servant will triumph (Isa. 52:13), for even though many will be shocked at his crucifixion (Isa. 52:14), this is nothing compared to the way kings will be stunned when he returns a second time (Isa. 52:15). So while he "made himself an offering for sin" so that this "seed" might live (Isa. 53:10), nevertheless, the Servant knew from eternity that the plan of the LORD would succeed" (Isa. 53:10).

The Son of Man

While there are additional pictures of the Messiah such as a "topstone" or "cornerstone" (Isa. 28:16; Zech. 3:9; 4:7; and Ps. 118:22), we conclude with Daniel's "Son of Man." This also is Messiah, but Messiah as reigning and ruling king. He will come one day "in the clouds of heaven" and there shall finally be given to him "dominion, and glory, and a kingdom, that all people, nations, and tongues, should serve him: his dominion is an everlasting dominion which shall not pass away, and his kingdom shall not be destroyed"(Dan. 7:13–14).

While modern scholarship is loathe to bring together the figures of the Servant of God and the Son of Man, neither Jesus nor some of his earlier predecessors at Qumran were at all hesitant to do so.[15] An obedient, serving, suffering "Son of Man" was not a contradiction in terms or mission, for it was all one person with one mission and a single plan: God's Messiah as announced in his everlasting promise.

1. Alfred Edersheim, *The Life and Times of Jesus the Messiah, II*, Grand Rapids: Eerdmans, 1953, Appendix IX, pp. 710–41. The distribution of the 456 O.T. passages was as follows: Pentateuch—75, Prophets—243, Writings—138.
2. The other four references of the nine are Ps. 20:6; 28:8; 84:9; and Hab. 3:13.
3. Willis J. Beecher. *The Prophets and The Promise*. Grand Rapids: Baker Book House, 1963, (r.p. of 1905), p. 376.

4. Ibid., p. 383
5. E. Jenni, "Messiah," *Interpreter's Dictionary of the Bible, III,* Nashville; Abingdon Press, 1962, p. 361.
6. R.A. Martin, "The Earliest Messianic Interpretation of Gen. 3:15," *Journal of Biblical Literature,* 84 (1965), pp. 425–27.
7. Charles A. Briggs, *Messianic Prophecy,* New York: Charles Scribner's Sons, 1889, pp. 82–83, note 1.
8. Henrikus Berkhof, *Christ The Meaning of History,* Richmond: John Knox Press, 1966, p. 153.
9. The view held by A. Kuenen, *The Prophets and Prophecy in Israel: An Historical and Critical Inquiry,* (tr. by Adam Milroy) London: Longmans, 1877, pp. 378–80, 456, 496 is well critiqued by Stanley Leanhes, *Old Testament Prophecy* (Warburton Lectures 1976–80), London: Hoddor and Stoughton, 1880, pp. 33–61. Also see the excellent article by O.T. Allis, "The Blessings of Abraham," *Princeton Theological Review* 25(1927),pp. 263–98. The meaning of the Hebrew Hitpa'el is often a simple passive (e.g. Prov. 31:30; Lam. 2:12; 4:1; Mic. 6:16; Ezek. 19:12). Surprisingly, even the cautious and conservative Franz Delitzsch, *Messianic Prophecies* (tr. by S.I. Curtiss), Edinburgh: T. & T. Clark, 1880, p. 31 rem. 3, takes the reflexive view because the passive meaning for the Hitpa'el is Late! Then he tries to slide the two views together and says "Since the nations will deserve the blessings of Abraham they will on that account be blessed . . . Spiritual blessings . . . fall to those who long for them"[!!].
10. Franz Delitzsch, p. 45.
11. Willis J. Beecher, pp. 346–48.
12. H.L. Ellison, *The Centrality of the Messianic Idea for the Old Testament,* London; Tyndale Press, 1953. On p. 16 he comments ". . . It is the more remarkable that there seems to be no trace at all of Moses' prophecy of a 'prophet like unto me' being interpreted messianically in rabbinic literature. In the New Testament it is used almost casually, as though its messianic meaning would be accepted without cavil . . ." Either it is suppressed or "The rabbis never thought through the relationship of the Messiah to the Law."
13. For development of this translation, see Walter C. Kaiser, Jr., "The Blessing of David: A Charter for Humanity," in *The Law and the Prophets: O.T. Allis Festschrift,* (ed. by J. Skilton), Phila.: Presbyterian and Reformed Pub. Co. 1973.
14. See Willis J. Beecher's excellent discussion, *The Prophets and The Promise,* pp. 263–88.
15. F.F. Bruce, *The New Testament Development of Old Testament Themes,* Grand Rapids: Eerdmans, 1968, pp. 88–99.

JEWISH PRACTICE AND IDENTITY IN THE BOOK OF ACTS

Lawrence J. Rich

"Judaism is for the Jew; Christianity is for the Gentile." This statement can be made before almost any group in our society and most people will agree. If it is suggested that a Jew can believe in Jesus and remain Jewish, it produces many raised eyebrows. Yet in the New Testament book of Acts the setting is quite the reverse. For over a decade following the resurrection and ascension of Jesus, his followers were almost exclusively Jewish. Believing in Jesus then was understood within the realm of Jewish faith and practice.

When Jesus was about to be lifted up to heaven (Acts 1:6–11), his mission was understood by his closest followers in connection with the Messianic kingdom promised to Israel. "Lord, is it at this time You are restoring the kingdom to Israel?" (1:6) Rather than responding that the coming of the kingdom to Israel would not happen, Jesus implied it would be postponed and that during the interim his followers should bring his message to others, beginning at Jerusalem.

It was on the day of Pentecost (the Jewish feast of Shavu'ot) that the Holy Spirit came upon the early Messianic believers (2:1–13), who apparently had come together in observance of the feast. Jewish people from many parts of the Roman Empire had come to Jerusalem for the feast and had now assembled together to consider the miraculous developments in the city that had resulted from the Spirit's work. Simon Peter, a leading Jewish follower of Jesus, explained the phenomenon to these assembled Jews in terms of Jewish prophecy and urged them to accept Jesus as the promised Messiah (2:14–40). Three thousand Jewish people accepted Jesus as Messiah in one day (2:41).

It was the practice at this time for Jesus' followers to go into the Temple at Jerusalem for worship and prayer (2:46; 3:1). On one such occasion, while on their way, they had an opportunity to heal a lame man and tell other Jewish people going to the Temple about Jesus the Messiah (3:2–26).

Soon the Messianic claims concerning Jesus became the talk of Jerusalem. The Sadducees, who were the ruling party and had political ties with the Roman authorities, were concerned that the threat of a king to rival Caesar would threaten their power (ch. 4). They threatened the believers not to preach the Messiahship of Jesus any more, but the disciples decided they could not abide by this requirement.

This Messianic faith continued to build an increasing allegiance among the Jewish people in Jerusalem, with quite a number of priests being included in the group of believers (6:7). At this time one of the disciples, Stephen, was particularly effective in preaching and in performing miracles. He was brought before the Council and gave a stirring defense of his faith in Jesus as the Messiah (ch. 7). During this entire period the setting was Jerusalem and the issues were Jewish ones—between Jews who believed the Messiah had come and those who did not.

Notable changes were ultimately to take place in the Messianic movement with the emergence on the scene of Saul of Tarsus. With the trial of Stephen (which was followed by his being stoned to death) a concerted effort began, led by Saul, to imprison the believers (8:3). Those who escaped were pursued by Saul as far north as Damascus. It is noteworthy that it was in the synagogues that these followers of Jesus were expected to be found (9:1–2). After Saul came to faith in Jesus he proclaimed the Messianic faith in those same synagogues (9:20).

Until then, the apostles were being consistent with the teachings of their Master, who had given them specific instructions when he sent out the twelve, as recorded in Matthew 10. For that mission the instructions had been clear: "Do not go in the way of the Gentiles, and do not enter any city of the Samaritans; but rather go to the lost sheep of the house of Israel" (Matt. 10:5–6). During the early post-resurrection years this continued to be the apostolic policy. As late as Acts 11:19 we are told, "So then those who were scattered because of the persecution that arose in connection with

Stephen made their way to Phoenicia and Cyprus and Antioch, speaking the word to no one except to Jews alone."

It was at this time that the Messianic faith began to include Gentiles. It came about through an act of divine intervention. A God-fearing centurion of Caesarea, named Cornelius, had a vision from the Lord indicating approval of his life of prayer and gifts of charity to the Jewish people. He was told to send for Simon Peter, who was lodging with a friend in Joppa, some forty miles south along the Mediterranean coast. As his representatives were nearing the house where Peter was staying, the apostle was at prayer. While waiting for a meal to be prepared, Peter had a vision of a sheet-like object being lowered from heaven. Upon this sheet were animals and birds which were forbidden to be eaten according to the Jewish dietary laws. Three times a voice came to him saying, "Arise, Peter, kill and eat." Each time Peter responded, "By no means, Lord, for I have never eaten anything unholy and unclean" (See ch. 10).

While Peter was reflecting on the vision, the men sent by Cornelius arrived, and the Holy Spirit told Peter to go with them. They explained that Cornelius had wanted him to come, and so Peter went with them. When he was in the house of Cornelius, where many people were assembled, Peter declared, "You yourselves know how unlawful it is for a man who is a Jew to associate with a foreigner or to visit him; and yet God has shown me that I should not call any man unholy or unclean" (10:28). It is significant that Peter did not understand the vision to mean that the practice of keeping kosher was wrong, but that it was not right to refuse to associate with a non-Jew. The outcome of this gathering was that Peter came to see that not only was the Messianic faith not for Jews only, but all people who repent of their sins and place their faith in the Messiah can find favor with God—a position reflected in Peter's statement to the group, "Of Him all the prophets bear witness that through His name every one who believes in Him has received forgiveness of sins" (10:43). This was divinely confirmed as the Holy Spirit came upon them all. Upon seeing this Peter ordered baptism (immersion) for them, declaring, "Surely no one can refuse the water for these to be baptized who have received the Holy Spirit just as we did, can he?" (10:47)

It was in Antioch in Syria that the movement of believing Gentiles gained momentum. Certain Jews came there and began speaking to non-Jews about believing in Jesus. Many responded in faith. Eventually the news reached Jerusalem, and the Messianic believers commissioned Barnabas to go to Antioch to view this development (11:22). Barnabas rejoiced at what he saw, encouraged these new believers, and saw many brought to faith. Remembering the gifted Saul who had returned to his home base of Tarsus, Barnabas went there, found Saul, and brought him to Antioch, where they taught the believers for a year. Eventually a large-scale Gentile mission developed from this, with Barnabas and Saul commissioned by the congregation at Antioch to go out into the Empire to spread the Word of salvation. Wherever they went preaching Jesus they made it their practice to go first to the synagogue.

The inclusion of Gentiles into the Messianic movement was a cause for rejoicing. Yet the nature of their standing and relationship to the Jewish believers and to Jewish practice became an issue. Did Gentiles need to practice the rituals of the Mosaic law? Was circumcision required? Because belief in Jesus was considered a Jewish faith, these were the natural questions that arose. Ultimately, a major gathering took place (the Council of Jerusalem) to consider these concerns and resolve the issue. At the Council Saul and Barnabas reported on the successful ministry they had been having with the Gentiles. But some of the Jewish believers stated, "It is necessary to circumcise them, and to direct them to observe the Law of Moses" (15:5). It is easy today to deride such a position, but the biblical grounds for such a statement were significant.

> Christians often fail to realize how strong a case this
> party had. When they used circumcision as the test
> of willingness to accept and observe the law of
> God, they chose their ground well. Genesis 17:9–
> 14 professes to quote the very words of God him-
> self, and God there commands that every
> descendant of Abraham, including foreigners who
> become members of his household, must practice
> circumcision "throughout your generations" as
> "an everlasting covenant." These, the very words of
> God, are given in authoritative Scripture; they must
> be observed. Gentiles are welcome in the church of

Christ, as the Jews widely welcomed proselytes to Judaism, but they must be circumcised, accept the Mosaic law, and observe the ceremonies it pre-scribes.[1]

There was much debate, after which Peter spoke up against placing such a yoke upon the Gentiles (15:7–11). Saul and Barnabas reviewed all that God had done through them among the Gentiles (15:12). Then James, who was the leader of the believers at Jerusalem, urged that the matter be resolved by not requiring the Gentiles to obey the Jewish law "but that we write to them that they abstain from things contaminated by idols and from fornication and from what is strangled and from blood" (15:20). James reminded his hearers that they need not fear the Law being forgotten or cast aside as it will continue to be declared each Sabbath in the synagogues (15:21). The apostles and elders deemed this a good way of resolving the matter, and the decision was to be spread to believers in Antioch and elsewhere.

A letter was drafted and carried to the congregation at Antioch, telling of the conclusions reached (15:22–29). "This is sometimes taken to mean that the entire Antioch church, including the Jewish Christians there, were freed from keeping any of the Mosaic law, but Acts 15:20, 29 and 21:25 refer only to Gentile Christians. The letter was directed to Gentile believers."[2]

Although this concession by the Jewish believers was made to the Gentile believers of that day, there are currently those who conclude that Jewish believers also are to abandon their traditions and practices. This is certainly not the conclusion of the Jerusalem Council. Rather, it was taken for granted that the Jewish believers would continue to practice their traditions, which they did, as the later record shows (21:20). "James expected Jews in the church to continue keeping the Mosaic law but he did not think it necessary to require Gentiles to do so."[3]

From that point on Saul (ultimately to be known as Paul) went throughout the Hellenistic world, speaking the good news of the Messiah to Jew and Gentile. At times significant numbers of Jews believed (17:12), some of them prominent (18:8). Although Paul spent much of his time with Gentiles, his identity and practice as a Jew remained visible. He observed the Jewish festivals, including

Passover and Shavu'ot/Pentecost (20:6, 16). He did not hesitate
to have Timothy circumcised, in deference to his countrymen
(16:3).

Upon returning to Jerusalem following his three missionary
journeys, Paul was told by James that there were thousands (literally tens of thousands) of Messianic Jews who were loyal to the
Jewish law and traditions (21:20). They had been hearing stories
about Paul—that he was encouraging Jewish believers among the
Gentile nations to forsake these things. Paul therefore was urged to
take a Nazirite vow in order to show "that there is nothing to the
things which they have been told about you, but that you yourself
also walk orderly, keeping the Law" (21:24); this Paul proceeded
to do (21:26). There are those who would say that this was an act
of expediency, but the record indicates no such thing. Rather, here
would have been the perfect opportunity for Paul to clear the air
on the place of the Jewish practices among Jewish believers. But
instead of speaking against the Law he chose to observe it.

In the late stages of Paul's career he continued to identify himself as a Jew who believed in the Messiah. "I am a Jew" (22:3), he
declared. "I am a Pharisee" (23:6), he stated. He suggested that a
purpose for his going to Jerusalem following his third missionary
journey was to go to the Temple for the purpose of worship
(24:11–12). He understood his faith within a Jewish framework
(24:14). He continued to observe Jewish practices (24:17–18).
The believers were classified by the authorities not as a new religion, but as a Jewish sect (24:5). Even as the book of Acts concludes, Paul (a prisoner) is seen speaking to Jewish leaders in Rome
(some believing and some not), reasoning from the Law and
Prophets, telling the Jews that he is imprisoned "for the sake of the
hope of Israel" (28:20), and having them refer to his faith not as an
entirely new movement or religion, but as a Jewish sect that is spoken of everywhere (28:22).

In studying the life of Paul some basic conclusions can be
drawn. First, Paul was a Jew not only by birth, but by lifestyle—
before and after his encounter with the Messiah. In the days of
Paul, Ellison tells us, for a man to be known as a Jew meant that he
kept the Law. However widely Jews differed, they all kept the Law.
The various sects within Judaism varied in their interpretation of
certain commandments, but in their actions they were remarkably

alike.[4] It is to be understood, therefore, that in the historical setting of the first century to deny the law in practice was to deny that one was a Jew.[5] There is reason to believe that Paul had the distinguishing dress of Diaspora Jews—the tassels or fringes on his outer garments as prescribed by Moses (cf. Num. 15:38ff). "That Paul was readily permitted to speak in a strange synagogue and even invited to do so (Acts 13:15) suggests that Paul proclaimed his Jewishness and even his rabbinic standing by his dress."[6]

Because daily practice (observance of the Law) was the characteristic mark of a Jew, and because Paul's activity was usually carried out in close proximity to the Jewish community, it can be seen that he was regularly being observed closely by Jewish leaders and authorities.

> There were really only two possibilities open to Paul. Either he did not observe the law at all, or he was strict in its observance at all times. A casual example of the latter is his keeping of the Day of Atonement under conditions when it might not have been expected. Yet Luke reports it in such a way as to show that he saw nothing remarkable in it (Acts 27:9).[7]
>
> So we are justified in thinking that throughout his missionary activity Paul lived in a way that would have called for no adverse comment from a Pharisee who might have met him however much he would have rejected his teaching.[8]

A second conclusion to be drawn is that Paul's message was perceived within a Jewish context rather than as a new faith. "When he told a Jew that he had found the long-promised Messiah, he appeared to his hearer as a Jew telling of a Jewish discovery."[9] In fact, according to W.D. Davies, "The Gospel for Paul was not the annulling of Judaism but its completion."[10] He clarifies further:

> Both in his life and thought, therefore, Paul's close relation to Rabbinic Judaism has become clear, and we cannot too strongly insist again that for him the acceptance of the Gospel was not so much the re-

jection of the old Judaism and the discovery of a
new religion wholly antithetical to it, as his polem-
ics might sometimes pardonably lead us to assume,
but the recognition of the advent of the true and
final form of Judaism, in other words, the advent of
the Messianic age of Jewish expectation.[11]

It is often assumed today that for a Jew to believe in Jesus is to
turn his back on his heritage and be "converted" to another religion. Paul never understood his faith in that way. Rather, in his
epistles, he spoke of the Gentiles as being grafted in to the Body of
Messiah (Rom. 11:17–24). The Gentiles are seen as coming into
the Messianic faith by accepting the Jewish Messiah. This helps
bring out the fact that there is not to be seen a contradiction between Paul's practice in Acts and his teaching in his epistles.[12]

The third conclusion that comes out of this study is that for
Paul, the Law of Moses is not cast aside, but rather is seen in a new
light. It is not the means by which one can attain salvation, but it
can be observed as a means of identity with the Jewish people and
of devotion to the God of Israel.

While relation with God is not to be gained by such
observance, certainly the liberty which is in Christ
allows the Christian to express that relation
through old forms which have been given a new
significance. At least it is evident that, from a religious perspective, the Jerusalem Christians still regarded the law as "an appropriate vessel into which
their own devotion could be poured."[13]

On a practical basis, Longenecker points out, "As members of
the remnant of Israel commissioned to call the rebellious sons of
Israel to repentance, they were duty bound to continue their practice of the Law if they were to remain in a position to gain a hearing
for their central message."[14] This is to be seen in contrast with historical Jewish evangelism, which has often de-emphasized Jewish
observance as being potentially Judaizing, and has therefore given
credence to the common viewpoint stated at the beginning, "Judaism is for the Jew and Christianity is for the Gentile."

If there can emerge in the public eye the comprehension that it is very much in order for a Jew to believe in Jesus and remain true to his heritage, then the blossoming of a New Testament-style Messianic movement can bring forth fruit for the Kingdom which will bring glory to the God of Israel and find many of the nation drawn into his fold.

1. Floyd V. Filson, *A New Testament History: The Story of the Emerging Church.* Philadelphia: The Westminster Press, 1964, pp. 214–215.
2. Ibid., p. 218.
3. Ibid.
4. H.L. Ellison, "Paul and the Law—'All Things to All Men'" in *Apostolic History and the Gospel* (Biblical and Historical Essays presented to F.F. Bruce on his 60th Birthday), edited by W. Ward Gasque and Ralph P. Martin, Grand Rapids: William B. Eerdmans Publishing Co., 1970, pp. 196–197.
5. Ibid., p. 200.
6. Ibid., p. 197.
7. Ibid., p. 198.
8. Ibid., p. 199.
9. Ibid., p. 200.
10. W.D. Davies, *Paul and Rabbinic Judaism: Some Rabbinic Elements in Pauline Theology.* New York and Evanston: Harper and Row, 1948, p. 323.
11. Ibid., p. 324.
12. Richard N. Longenecker, *Paul, Apostle of Liberty: The Origin and Nature of Paul's Christianity.* Grand Rapids: Baker Book House, 1964, pp. 260–3.
13. Longenecker, p. 281.
14. Ibid., p. 281.

COVENANT, FULFILLMENT, AND JUDAISM IN HEBREWS

Hebrews has long been viewed as a dynamic treatise demonstrating how Yeshua fulfills the Old Testament and Judaism. Judaism and the Old Testament are then often viewed as beautiful pictures of his character and functions but as having been set aside with the advent of Yeshua. The argument goes something like this. "Judaism pointed to Yeshua the Messiah. When he came, died and rose, he fulfilled the Jewish system. Therefore, it is no longer relevant, having been set aside because it fulfilled its function of pointing to the Messiah. So, using Jewish elements of faith or worship means going back to 'the old life.' It involves placing oneself 'under the law,' going back to a system opposed to God's gracious operations through Yeshua. This contradicts its fulfillment in him."[1]

But should Hebrews be so understood? In order to interpret Hebrews correctly, we need to understand its background and setting. This includes the nature of covenant in the Near East, the nature of fulfillment in Scripture, and the nature of the people and beliefs being addressed by the epistle. Proper treatment of the crucial passages in Hebrews necessitates such preliminary study.

The Nature of Covenant in the Near East

Great similarities exist between biblical covenant passages, e.g. Exodus 20ff. and Deuteronomy, and the Hittite treaties of the fourteenth and thirteenth centuries B.C.E. While we also have examples of later treaties, the biblical texts definitely correspond to these earlier ones.[2] They exhibit an identical structure and sequence of elements.

1. Preamble, identifying the initiator of the covenant; Exod. 20:1; Deut. 1:1–5.
2. Historical prologue, specifying the previous relationship that existed between the covenanting parties; Exod. 20:2; Deut. 1:6–3:29.
3. Stipulations, the obligations involved both
a. general; Exod. 20:3–17, 22–26; Deut. 4–11; and
b. specific; Exod. 21–23, 25–31; Lev. 1–25; Deut. 12–26.
4. Arrangements for
a. placing a copy of the treaty in the sanctuary of the parties' gods; Exod. 25:16; Deut. 31:9, 24–26; and
b. regular public readings of the treaty; Deut. 31:10–13.
5. Witnesses, invoked to witness the treaty; Deut. 4:26; 30:19; 31:28; Exod. 24:4; Deut. 31:26.
6. Curses and blessings, based on fulfillment of the stipulations:
a. blessings; Lev. 26:3–8; Deut. 28:1–14;
b. curses: Lev. 26:14–33; Deut. 28:15–68.
7. Oath of obedience and ratifying ceremony; Exod. 24:1–11; Deut. 27; 29:10, 12.[3]

Treaties such as these were not parity treaties, treaties made between equals. They were called suzerainty treaties, treaties between a great king and a vassal nation. In these the vassal entered into an oath of loyalty and trust to the king out of gratitude for benefits already received.[4] Thus, the treaty served as a declaration of the lordship of the great king over his servant people. It, therefore, included certain obligations to the king because of his leadership, protection and goodness. The past generosity of the king formed the basis for gratitude and future obedience. The historical prologue served as an encouragement and reminder of this. It was designed to inspire confidence and gratitude and to encourage the people to keep their covenant obligations.

By nature the covenant, or treaty, formed a legal relationship. Thus it became a strong guarantee of a continuing relationship. "Shalom" described the relationship, one of wholeness and harmony. So the covenant was intended to bring about a state of orderliness and rightness between the two parties, making possible a good relationship in things pertaining to everyday life.[5]

This kind of covenant relationship implied certain things. The establishing of the covenant resulted in God's rule over Israel. Israel's promise of obedience was an acknowledgement of his authority.[6] The Near Eastern covenant applied to all of life, from everyday life to the largest of matters. Since God rules as king, all of life—everyday affairs, major matters, even religious life—is under his direction. This makes for a holistic perspective. The ancient Israelite did not then segment life into our modern religious and secular distinctions. All was included in living under the king.[7]

The covenant alone distinguished between people dealt with by force and those according to normal peaceful procedures. It served as a line of demarcation. Those under covenant enjoyed peaceful interaction with the sovereign. Those outside were dealt with by force. Violation of covenant obligations usually implied moving into a "no-covenant" state.[8] On the other hand, peace and blessing indicated that the covenant was still in force. It had not been broken; it was being carried through; the relationship still continued.

The fundamental function of the covenant was to establish a community of interest between the king and his vassals.[9] Covenant thus implies community—the forming of common customs, common views, a common life. This meant an intimate sharing of life, nature and custom, with the wills of the contracting parties ultimately becoming identical. This commonness of will implied in the covenant showed that the parties had united for a common aim; they had become part of a close union. The closer the union, the more intercommunication of personality occurred, something akin to the biblical concept of "becoming whole with" another (cf. 1. Kings 8:61, "perfect with"). When this happened, the stronger imparted his character to the relationship, and the weaker united to enjoy his strength.[10] So, God's will and purpose were to stamp the relationship between God and Israel,

At its core, love forms the key to the covenant relationship. The historical prologue shows this quite clearly. It points to the gracious actions of the king prior to the covenant and in initiating it, and specifies this as the foundation of the relationship. There had been a powerful demonstration of his love, the Exodus (cf. Deut. 1:1–8:4). This had been preceded by his love to Israel's

ancestors (Deut. 4:37; 7:7–11; 10:15). As love initiated the relationship, so it was to permeate the whole of its continuation.
Love and gratitude were to infect all of life and thinking under
the covenant. In fact, Deuteronomy 5–11 can be seen as an emphasis on whole-hearted love toward God, with the stress being
laid not on the ability to do but on the will to fulfill the covenant
obligations. Deuteronomy 6:4–6 provides the classic expression
of this wholehearted love which was expected as Israel's response.
The passage calls for exclusive devotion and commitment to God
alone, a love expressed through the entire being and personality.
It also involves a total pattern of life. Deuteronomy 12–25, for
example, provides the guidelines for this pattern of living. They
provide concrete expressions of love and devotion to God and its
natural consequence, love for others.[11] Deuteronomy 10:20
highlights this emphasis on love. It uses the same word "cleave"
as found in Genesis 2:24. In both cases "cleave" indicates a love
relationship. Obedience without love is possible—think, for example, of the army—but not so love without obedience. If a person truly loves, he will obey and attempt to please. Marriage
provides a good example. When it works properly, love is the key-
note. If it falls apart, it ends up in court, where everything is done
on a legalistic basis. (But in Deuteronomy, even in exile and judgment, God promises his love and mercy.) When any free-will relationship breaks down, then rules become important and legalism
results.[12] So love, not law, forms the core of the covenant relationship between God and Israel.

The historical pattern of the Near Eastern treaty shows that it
was not obedience to the Law which resulted in the covenant and a
relationship with God. The historical pattern involved a miraculous deliverance, the Exodus, an example of God's grace. Then a
covenant was made and a relationship was formalized, again at
God's initiative. Hengstenberg perceptively notes that in essence
the covenant legally formalized an already existing relationship
rather than actually establishing one (cf. Exod. 6:6–8 and the use
of the historical prologue in the treaties).

> The substance of the covenant evidently precedes
> the outward conclusion of the covenant, and forms
> the foundation of it. The conclusion of the cov-

enant doesn't first form the relation but is merely a solemn acknowledgement of the relation already existing. Thus it is ever in human relation; the contract, as a rule, only fixes and settles outwardly, a relation already existing. And that is still more the case in the relations between God and man.[13]

Only after all this—the Exodus and the formalizing of the covenant relationship—did the ordinances or stipulations follow. They provided guidelines in maintaining the relationship and indicated what was expected of one in covenant relationship with God.[14]

Therefore, Torah should not be viewed as a law code. (In fact, the Hebrew means "instruction," and not law.)[15] Law codes existed in Moses' time and could have served as a pattern for the biblical texts. The explicit covenant formulation of Exodus and Deuteronomy stands as strong, direct evidence that this is a treaty or covenant and not a code of law. It is a declaration of God's kingship and his choice of a people for himself. A people related to God the king were to live a sovereignly designated order of life, for which they received instructions, the Torah. The designated order of life was important for good communications and an orderly relationship. When a people entered into a covenant relationship they gratefully took on certain obligations, the instructions which served as a guide for the covenant order of life.[16] There is a basic, underlying principle: benefits bestowed, or a relationship entered, logically implies consequent responsibilities or obligations.

In all the covenants of the Old Testament (including the promised "New Covenant") the establishment of the *relationship* precedes the outward conclusion of the covenant and is independent of its acknowledgement. After God has established a relationship by his grace and man has responded by accepting God's gift of love as it is visualized in the covenant form and specified by the promise context of the covenant, God rightfully expects a life which exhibits this believer's new life in the Man of Promise. Even in the so-called unconditional covenants made with Noah (Gen. 9:9) and Abraham (Gen.

12, 15), the covenant imposes upon those who receive it certain implicit and explicit obligations
which are afterwards repeated and amplified.[17]

The Near Eastern treaty pattern thus bears directly on our understanding of the essence of Torah. Essentially, the great king
granting the treaty says: "These are all the things I've done for you.
You didn't deserve them, but I did them nevertheless. Now, because of your gratitude and love, I expect you to be faithful to me
and to my government. Here's how you can be faithful and demonstrate your love; these are my guidelines." So the concept of covenant shows that all of the Torah material must be understood as
the grace of God. He established the nation and the covenant relationship by grace, and he graciously provided guidelines for expressing that relationship through love and loyalty.

Before investigating the significance of the renewal procedure
of Near Eastern covenants, it would be important to take a "second
look" at the New Covenant. The prophets also refer to it as the
everlasting covenant or covenant of peace (cf. Jer. 32:40; Ezek.
16:60; Isa. 54:10; 55:3, *et. al.*). Cullmann has already noted the
dynamic interplay of old and new, past and present.

> That the past is never simply the past is shown ev-
> erywhere . . . The past is seen as salvation-history in
> the light of the present, but the present cannot be
> recognized at all as salvation-history without the
> positive presentation of the past. . . . Salvation-his-
> tory forms a whole that as such remains ever
> present.[18]

But does this interplay account completely for Jeremiah 31? It
seems quite possible that Jeremiah intended the New Covenant to
be viewed as a *renewed* covenant.[19] A number of the associated passages (Ezek. 16:60ff; Isa. 55:3; Mic. 7:18–20, and especially Jer.
33:14–22) appear to indicate that this covenant is a ratification of
the previous covenants with Abraham, Moses and David.[20] In this
sense alone, the New Covenant can be viewed as a renewal. A number of writers have seen this, e.g. Calvin and Hengstenberg.

The New Covenant so flowed from the old, that it was almost the same in substance while distinguished in form.[21]

The New Covenant which is to take the place of the Old, when looking to the form (comp. Heb. 8:13), is in substance, the realization of the Old. These remarks are in perfect harmony with that which was formerly said concerning the meaning of *make a covenant.* We saw that this expression does not designate an act only once done, when a covenant is solemnly sanctified, but rather that it is used of every action by which a covenant relation is instituted or confirmed.[22]

Further, as Kaiser points out,[23] the Hebrew and Greek terms for "new" used with this covenant frequently mean "renew," or "restore," as can be seen in the phrases "new moon," "new heart," and "new heavens and earth."

Many scholars have noted that there is very little "new" in this covenant; many of its specifics have been mentioned under earlier covenants, e.g.

1. God's law;
2. "I will be their God and they will be my people" (cf. Gen. 17:7; Exod. 6:7);
3. "They will know the Lord" (cf. Exod. 6:7, et. al);
4. Complete forgiveness of sin (cf. Exod. 34:6–7; Ps. 103:12; Mic. 7:18f);
5. Even possibly the creation of a new heart (cf. Ps. 51:12).

Each of the items adduced is but a repetition of some familiar aspect of salvation already known in the Old Testament.[24]

Can the New Covenant, then, in any sense claim to be new? Jeremiah may be using "new" in an ironical way, much as he uses irony elsewhere in his prophecy.[25] Israel should have been experiencing these "new" realities, but they weren't. To shock them out of complacency Jeremiah suggests that God will establish a new covenant as if these realities were foreign to them. Their experience of these realities would be as radical as a new covenant. Jeremiah

intended this treatment to lead the complacent person to realize
that he was not experiencing the realities of a relationship with
God. Wallis finds confirmation of this in the same use of irony in
the New Testament with respect to the New Covenant.

> Probably the most transparent of these New Testa-
> ment cases is found in Galatians 4:21ff. Already the
> note of irony is heard in Paul's words, "Tell me,
> you who desire to be under law . . ." Verse 24
> brings the apparently straightforward statement,
> "these women are two covenants." However, in the
> subsequent development and contrast of the two
> covenants, Paul's irony becomes apparent. The one
> covenant corresponding to Sarah and leading on to
> the mention of liberty, and climaxed by the quota-
> tion from Isaiah 54, is clearly the covenant of salva-
> tion by grace. By contrast, the mention of the other
> covenant with its accompaniments of slavery, and
> most pointedly the slavery of the "present Jerusa-
> lem," make it plain that Paul is equating this other
> covenant with the Christ-rejecting Judaism of his
> day. Now to call this latter situation a "covenant" is
> surely ironical for Paul. Paul certainly intends an
> emphatic rejection of it by his hearers. In the para-
> bolic words "cast out the slave and her son . . . Paul
> means to say that the specious appeal of legalism to
> Moses is not a real covenant, but is the very antith-
> esis of it—a broken covenant, as Jeremiah phrased
> it. . . .
>   The theme of two covenants emerges in II
> Corinthians 3:14–15. "But their minds were hard-
> ened; for to this day, when they read the old cov-
> enant the same veil remains unlifted, because only
> through Christ is it taken away. Yes, to this day
> whenever Moses is read a veil lies over their minds.
> . . ." Paul apparently does not mean by "old cov-
> enant" the volume of 24 books, *simpliciter.* He
> clearly means that Christ is in the Old Testament.
> In Romans 10:6–10, quoting Deuteronomy

30:12–13, Paul is careful to say that Moses' message is his message—"the word of faith which we preach." It is Moses as read with hardened mind and veiled heart which is called the "old covenant." "Old Covenant" is a way to express what happens when unbelief reads the book. Clearly we are hearing Jeremiah's note of irony: the "old covenant" implied in Jeremiah's promise of a "new covenant" is Moses read with eyes which do not see Christ: the "new covenant" is not really "new"; it is only a true exegesis of Moses. The newness of the covenant is subjective and psychological: in Jeremiah's terms, it is the writing of the law on the heart. When the heart turns to the Lord, the veil is removed and the glories of salvation by grace shine on every page. Believers, beholding with unveiled face and heart, see the glory of Christ.[26]

In wrestling with the same problems, Hengstenberg takes a different tack, stressing the internal and the deeper as the newness.

The point in question cannot be a new and more perfect revelation of the Law of God; for that is common to both the dispensations. No jot or tittle of it can be lost under the New Testament, and as little can a jot or tittle be added. God's Law is based on His nature, and that is eternal and unchangeable, compare Malachi 3:22 (4:4). . . . As little can the discourse be of the introduction of an entirely new relation, which is not founded at all upon the former one. On this subject, David Kimchi's remark is quite pertinent: "It will not be the newness of the covenant, but its stability." The covenant with Israel is an everlasting covenant. Jehovah would not be Jehovah, if an entirely new commencement could take place—so the Apostle writes in Romans 15:8. The Law is the same; the relation only is different in which God places it to man.[27]

Great depth, stability and internality appear as key elements of newness. In fact, after reviewing the different items in the New Covenant and showing that they were in place under the "old covenant," he concludes: "We have thus before us merely a difference in degree."[28] The degree, extent and depth of the experience of God are much richer and fuller. As Hebrews 10 adds, worshippers now have a "cleansed conscience" because of the finality and completeness of Yeshua's sacrifice. Comparing Yeshua's statements in John 14:16–17 with the New Covenant promise of Ezekiel 36:25–27, the *permanency* of the Spirit's indwelling appears as new also, enabling us to partake of God's nature, making his Torah an internal motivating principle of our natures and enabling us to carry out its instructions (Rom. 8:4).

> "And I will give my Law in the inward parts. . ."
> The Law is the expression of God's nature; it is only
> by the Law being written in the heart that man can
> become a partaker of God's nature: that His name
> can be sanctified in him.[29]

The repeated violations of his covenant make this statement stand even more beautifully as an expression of God's grace. Despite the broken covenant, he renews the terms and grants even greater blessing. He then takes it all one step further, extending the scope of the covenant. *All* people (Jer. 31:34) will participate in its provisions—perhaps another element of its newness.

A resolution to the problem of newness apparently lies in a combination of Wallis' and Hengstenberg's insights. However, one other perspective needs to be added to complete the picture, the implications of the Near Eastern covenant renewal procedure. When the covenants were renewed, new documents were prepared, which *brought up to date* the stipulations of the earlier documents. Deuteronomy illustrates this process (Deut. 5:6–21; 15:5ff; cf. Exod. 12:7,4). It provides evidence for the fact that this was a renewal of the earlier covenant at the point in time when the leadership was transfered to Joshua. It *includes* the stipulations and sanctions of the original covenant. It is, in fact, the text of the treaty reproduced, as was common in the ancient Near East, for the dynastic succession of Joshua.[30] Joshua followed the same procedure when he took leave of the people (Josh. 24:55ff). So, it served not only as a renewal of the covenant, but also as the testament or will of Moses, making Joshua his successor. This correlates directly with the statements of Hebrews 9:17–17, emphasizing the necessity for the death of the testator to affect the covenant.

> From the viewpoint of the subject people the treaty guaranteeing the suzerain's dynastic succession is an expression of the covenant relationship to their overlord; but from the viewpoint of the royal son of the suzerain the arrangement is testamentary . . . it is not in force while the testator lives.[31]

Kline goes on to point out that Yeshua dies as the representative of God, putting the testament into effect. He then rises as the heir, succeeding to the throne. Yeshua's reticence to proclaim himself the Messianic king may reflect this perspective.[32]

In addition to the perspectives of irony, internality, enabling, extent and renewal as they relate to the New Covenant, the principle of Galatians 3:17 applies to any covenant discussion. One covenant does not set aside another. One does not invalidate another so as to nullify its stipulations. Rather, it renews, expands, adapts, updates. Jocz reminds us of one further aspect, a tension which Hebrews 8:13 also hints at in its use of the present tense. Building upon Cullman, he notes:

> . . . though the "old has passed away and new has come," yet "the past remains real, everlasting and unrelinquishable." This interplay of past and present, new and old derives from the fact that history is still an on-going process: we therefore have to say both: "already and not yet."[33]

The Nature of Fulfillment in the Bible

The fulfillment theme in Hebrews maintains the divine origin and establishment of the Jewish system. Rather than manifesting an attitude of disparagement or annulment, Hebrews hallows, reveres and makes prominent, as Westcott noted.

Prominence is assigned in the epistle to the Old Testament, both to the writing and to the institutions it hallows. There is not the least tendency towards disparagement of the one or the other. . .

From first to last it is maintained that God spoke to the fathers in the prophets. The message through the son takes up and crowns all that had gone before.[34]

So, Judaism foreshadows Yeshua as it is fulfilled in and highlights him. He takes it up in himself, and crowns, fills out and gives meaning to the Jewish system. This cannot be adequately seen if the Jewish system, the "highlighter," is removed from the picture. It is not set aside but serves as a good contemporary teacher pointing to Yeshua. Set the system aside, and you remove the pointer.

Anyone who quotes scripture such as Galatians 4:8–10, Colossians 2:16–17, or Romans 14:5–6 to prove that the Jewish festivals or holy days are forbidden to Jewish believers in Yeshua is reading the Bible entirely out of context. Paul is not addressing Jewish believers who are celebrating these days in the name of Yeshua; therefore, his words cannot be taken as criticism of believers who are celebrating these days in the name of Yeshua. The Jewish festivals foreshadow the Messiah and are fulfilled in him. However, a shadow cannot highlight anyone, even the Messiah, if it is totally removed from the picture.[35]

The objection usually comes at this point. "The argument of Hebrews demonstrates that the new is better than the old; so the old is set aside." But Hebrews applies the same argument to angels as to the old covenant. If the old is set aside and void, by the same argument the angels must be as well!

Yeshua's teachings in Matthew 5:17–19 shed further light on the meaning of fulfillment. He uses "abolish" and "fulfill" as opposites here. The Greek term used, *kataluo*, conveys the idea of "do away with," "annul," "make invalid," or "repeal."[36] Yeshua did not come to do this to the Jewish system. In fact, he mentions "not abolish" twice to emphasize his point. The Greek construction connecting "not abolish" and "fulfill" (*ouk . . . alla*) indicates a strong contrast. It reinforces the opposite nature of the two ideas, implying that one contradicts the other. They are thus shown as mutually exclusive.

The word "fulfill" (*pleroo*) carries a variety of nuances: (a) make full, fill full, fill out fully; (b) make complete, confirm; (c) show forth in its true meaning, bring to full expression. The prominent idea here is "bring to full expression," "show forth in its true meaning."[37] And, as the context brings out (v. 20ff), the idea of "fill out fully" also plays a significant role.

> The old law remains. The New Testament does not bring any new law, but does apply the old in the light of the fulfillment of the salvation-history. Even in the Sermon on the Mount Jesus brings no new law, but shows how in each situation the old Law is to be fulfilled radically in view of the Kingdom of God which is immeasurably closer.[38]

Further, as Beecher reminds us, the Bible presents fulfillment as cumulative, not disjunctive.[39] The passage conveys the image of a crown. A crown shows something off in its full radiance. The whole Jewish system foreshadows Yeshua and highlights him, emphasizing his brilliance and glory. He, in turn, takes it up in himself and crowns it; he fills it and gives it meaning. He shows it off in its full radiance and significance.

We can conclude, then, that Yeshua came as the fullest expression of the Jewish system, thoroughly consistent with it in its pure form, as the central, integral, and essential part of it. He showed us its true meaning and lifted it to new heights (cf. its previous heights in Ps. 19, 119). He crammed it full to the brim.

The Nature of the People and Beliefs Addressed by Hebrews

Scholars have frequently argued about the kind of people addressed by the author of Hebrews. Some have made a case for a Gentile audience, while others have argued for a Jewish one. Both positions have their problems.

> The main problem in identifying the nature of the addressees has been the very strange combination of beliefs which the readers are urged not to return to or exhorted to move away from. What Jewish group would have held to a theology that combined the veneration of angels, Mosaic prophetology, the exaltation of Melchizedek, the portrayal of the cultus in terms of the wilderness tabernacle, and the vital importance of the sacrifice system . . .[40]

This combination does not fit the Pharisees or Sadducees, for example. The priesthood and cultus as concepts of importance would be alien to Pharisees, as angels and the tabernacle would be to the Sadducees.[41] However, Melchizedek as a main theme is perhaps the most problematic to assign to a Jewish group. He plays a very prominent role in Hebrews (especially chapters 5–7), but has little or no significance for the commonly known Jewish sects. The Dead Sea community at Qumran (probably Essenes) stands as the one exception. Melchizedek figured prominently in their thinking. He had a heavenly position and played an active role as an eschatological savior. Identified with the Messiah in some way, he was expected to come to proclaim release to the captives and atonement for their sins. Anointed by the Spirit, he would punish the wicked in the last days[42] (Cf. 11QMel[43]). A closer examination of the beliefs addressed in Hebrews and a comparison with the Qumran teachings demonstrates their close relationship and argues for an Essene-type audience for Hebrews.

The following analysis depends on the work of Yigael Yadin.[44]

As deduced from the argument of Hebrews, its readers believed that angels would play an important role in the last days. They would operate under the direct order of God and not as servants to a Messianic agent (1:6–7, 14). In the world to come they would possess certain controlling powers and dominion (1:13; 2:1ff). Their status would be such that they would possess some sort of qualities of sonship in relation to God (1:5ff). In comparison, the Essenes believed that the angel of light, Michael, would assist the "children of righteousness." His authority would be magnified, and he would have dominion over the "children of light" (1QM 13.9–10; 1QS 3.20, 24–25). Angels, in general, would have controlling powers, and God would operate through them directly (1QH 10.8, 1QH Fragment 2, 1.3). The scrolls also speak of angels as sons of heaven or sons of God (1QH Fragment 2,1.3; 1QH 3.122; 1QS 11.7–8).

The readers of Hebrews expected a Messianic priest figure or a priestly Messiah, specifically from the tribe of Aaron (5:1f). He would rival or be superior to Messiah the king (7:18). He would oversee a restored and purified sacrificial system, which would be primary in importance, as well as efficacious (10:lff; 9:25–26). Similarly, those at Qumran recognized a Messiah "from Aaron" as well as one "from Israel," a priestly Messiah and a kingly one (CDC 12.22; 13.1; 14.19; 20.1; 1QS 11.11). The priestly Messiah would assume a leading role over the kingly one in the conduct of the war against the enemy, and both would serve under Michael (1QM). The scrolls call this priestly Messiah "the chief priest" and "prince of the whole congregation" (1QM 5.1; CDC 7.18–21; 1QS 3.20–21). The full ritual of the sacrifices would be resumed in prominence in the last days under the direction of the chief priest and would provide atonement for the congregation (1QM 2.1–6).

In the last days the readers of Hebrews looked for a prophet, separate from the Messiah, to appear with a new revelation (1:1–2, cf. the stress on Yeshua as the *final* revelation and on his superiority to the *prophets)*. This probably reflects the widespread belief in the eschatological role of the "prophet like Moses" (Deut. 18:18ff. cf. Matt. 16:14; James 6:14). This Mosaic prophet apparently had some connection with the New Covenant (9:15ff.). The Dead Sea community believed in the coming of a prophet separate from the two Messiahs: ". . . until the coming of a prophet and of the Messiahs from Aaron and Israel" (1QS 9.11). They apparently considered him a "second Moses," and as such perhaps expected him to serve as the mediator of the New Covenant between God and Israel (cf. the beginning of *Assumption of Moses)*.

Hebrews frequently refers to biblical passages about the tabernacle—which was quite distinct from the Temple system—and the wilderness wanderings (chs. 3–4, 9–10 etc.). The repeated references to the wilderness tabernacle are quite striking because the readers lived in Temple days over a thousand years after the wilderness tabernacle. Apparently, the author tries to prove his points by using concepts close to the readers' outlook and understood by them. So, he shows that Yeshua fulfills important aspects of the tabernacle (ch. 9ff.). Significantly, the Qumran community organized themselves as a replica of the tribes of Israel in the wilderness. (Cf. 1QM, 1QS, and CDC on the entire following discussion.) They called their leaders by the same titles as those in Exodus, and their age requirements for service in the congregation and in war correspond to those in Numbers. They referred to themselves as "exiles in the wilderness" and believed they would enter a new land of promise. While they awaited this, they imitated Israel's pattern of life in the wilderness. They were, therefore, quite familiar with the tabernacle and partial to it. They used the same measurements for their weapons as those given for the tabernacle furniture. Because they felt the existing Temple and its services were defiled by the corruption and present order of the priesthood, they viewed the tabernacle system as purer.

A couple other notes should be added about the nature of those addressed by Hebrews. The strong emphasis on the New Covenant (chs. 8–10) may also reflect a background of Essene beliefs. The Essenes felt that they were members of the New Covenant (CDC 6.19; 8.21; 20.12).[45] In fact, yearly they celebrated the renewing of this covenant on Shavu'ot (Pentecost).[46] The Essenes also would have felt right at home with the stress on the end of days (cf. 1QM) found right at the outset of Hebrews (1:2). Finally, if Hebrews was written in the tense period before the revolt against Rome, the Messianic Jews were facing a difficult choice and test of loyalty either to their nation or their Messiah. The author wants them not to revert to a Judaism without the Messiah.[47]

Now that we have examined the nature of covenant in the Near East, the nature of fulfillment in the Bible, and the nature of the people and beliefs addressed by Hebrews, we are better prepared to analyze the crucial passages in the book of Hebrews.

The Crucial Passages in Hebrews

Although not usually so interpreted, some have used Hebrews 6:1–2 as an attack on Judaism and Jewish identity.

> It is evident that the elementary teaching about the Messiah is Old Testament Judaism and was no longer operative because the fulfillment had come. Thus, "let us go on!"[48]

But is this so evident? Westcott, for example,[49] equates the elementary teaching with the first teaching of the apostles (cf. Acts 2:38; 4:2, 33; 8:16f.). The context (5:11f.) reinforces Westcott's understanding and militates against the former interpretation. The context equates "elementary teaching" with milk, those first principles which fed the young believers. These are necessary for early growth but are inadequate to fuel further development. As a person grows properly, he grows beyond the ABCs and moves on to that which assists his maturity. As Bruce[50] restyles the author's point: You have remained immature long enough; I am going to give you something which will take you out of your immaturity. The "milk" and the ABCs do not pertain solely to Jewish teachings but apply more broadly to basic teachings given to new believers in general, as the context indicates. To this Westcott adds an important perspective.

> We hold what we have as a preparation for something more. At the same time all that is surrendered is incorporated in that which is afterward gained. In relation to the Hebrews the word *aphentes* has the sense of "leave" as applied to those who advance to a deeper knowledge.
>
> The writer does not (of course) mean to say that his readers must build higher without having secured their foundation.[51]

Besides, who in his right mind would want to abandon such teachings as "faith toward God" and "the resurrection of the dead" in a mad rush to maturity? Hebrews 6 challenges us to build on these, not abandon them.

Hebrews 8 poses a more difficult problem. The passage speaks of a better covenant and better promises (vv. 6, 13). Apparently this sets aside the old, doing away with the Jewish system, as some would assert. Note first though, the passage speaks of a "better covenant" and "better promises," not a better Torah. God's Torah could not be improved, as Galatians 3:21 implies. Besides, how could you improve on something God describes as "holy, just and good," and as "spiritual" (Rom. 7:12, 14)? Further, Yeshua clearly stated that he fulfilled, not set aside, the Torah. Hebrews would not contradict this clear teaching.

To what, then, do the better promises and better covenant refer? Clearly the reference involves a *covenant* and *promises*. From the context they refer to the *New Covenant promise* of the Torah on the heart (v. 10). This is the new dimension of the covenant—internality and enabling. However, it is based on the same Torah; it has just been internalized, not set aside. It is no longer simply an objective criterion outside the believer. It invades him as his very essence, driving force and motivating impulse from within. This fits the conclusions of our survey on Near Eastern covenant procedure. Jeremiah spoke in ironical terms about the "new" covenant whereby the people would experience the kind of intimate relationship with God he intended for them under the previous covenants. So it was really a renewed covenant, ratifying the past covenants and enabling its participants to experience the intended benefits. As in the Near East with the renewal of covenants, here also the relationship and obligations continued but were brought up to date (as for example, the Sermon on the Mount, which explains, adapts and expands the Torah). The dimension of enabling and internality remains as the striking "newness" of the covenant.

> The new covenant was to be better than the old one because the people would be enabled to keep it. It would be written on the minds and hearts rather than on tables of stone.[52]

Verse 7 goes on to state that the first covenant was not faultless. But as the context demonstrates (vv. 8–9), the problem resides not with the covenant, promises or Torah, but with man. He "finds fault with [blames] them" (v. 8) because "*they* did not continue in my covenant" (v. 9). Or, as Jeremiah put it (31:32), "which covenant *they broke.*" To this, Romans 8:3 adds that it was "weak because of the flesh." The passages emphasize man's inability to keep the covenant. This perspective is emphasized by the terms in verses 7 and 8. "Faultless"—referring to the covenant—and "blaming"—referring to man—come from the same root, making the point that the covenant was not blameless because the Jewish people could not keep it.[53]

Verse 13 adds the phrases "obsolete," "growing old" and "ready to disappear." Once again these refer to the covenant, not to the Torah, and do so because of the new dimension. Further, the term "obsolete" means "outdated" or "antiquated," not "annulled." The new dimension makes the former covenant antiquated. The believer, by the Spirit of God, can now accomplish what before he was commanded but was not able to carry out. Thus, there is now a better way to accomplish the same old objectives. (Romans 8:4 proclaims the same message.)

Notice, too, that verse 13 says "growing old" and "ready to disappear," not "old" and "having disappeared." The former still has a present use. This reflects the "already and not yet" tension expressed by Jocz and the interplay of old and new noticed by Cullmann, as cited earlier. The ultimate fulfillment of the "new" awaits the Messianic age when "everyone shall know God" (v. 11) and "the Torah will go forth from Zion" (Isa. 2:3).[54]

Hebrews 9:3–10 poses still another problem for continuance of Jewish practice and identity, particularly verse 10, which seems to indicate an end for the "regulations of food and drink and various washing." Clearly, the context (vv. 7, 9, 12–13, 19) refers to the sacrifice system that existed in both tabernacle and Temple. The main point of the passage occurs in verse 8: "the way into the holy place hadn't yet been disclosed." In other words, the people had no direct, unhindered, free access to God within that structure. ". . . the people were separated from the object of their devotion."[55] So, the author contrasts the free access to God with the symbolic limited access permitted to the tabernacle and the Temple.[56] Verse 9 explains verse 8 and then verse 10 modifies verse 9, thus continuing the expansion of verse 8. Therefore, the regulations of food, drink and washings in verse 10 refer to those associated with the sacrifice system and not to the food laws, other washings, et al., ". . . the accompaniments of the sacrifice, the personal requirements with which they were connected . . . "[57] These regulations relating to the sacrifices were temporary, as was the sacrificial system. However, as the text notes (v. 9), even this was a picture or lesson for "the present time" ("then" is not in the Greek text); it served a present function.

The text concludes by stating that the regulations were imposed until a time of "reformation" or "new order." The term "reformation" used here implies reconstruction[58] or renewal, as opposed to building a new structure. It means "making straight," the idea of making stable,[59] reminiscent of Kimchi's statement cited earlier: "It will not be the newness of the covenant, but its stability." Qumran, too, eagerly anticipated this time of the *renewal* of creation after final judgment.[60] This verse refers to the time initiated by Yeshua, with his one *permanent* sacrifice replacing the many *temporary* ones (as chapters 9 and 10 go on to develop).

Hebrews 13:10–14 stands as the last major, crucial passage relating to Jewish continuity. Verse 13 expresses the key to the paragraph, "bearing his reproach." It states the only command in the section, "go to him outside the camp." "Bearing his reproach" then modifies the command, explaining its meaning. The command emphasizes identifying with Yeshua: "go to him . . ." So the author stresses not leaving behind, but identifying with Yeshua, even if it means reproach and persecution. The Dead Sea community, and those influenced by it, would have understood reproach because of the stand they had taken in separating themselves. To them, Hebrews says: "Now suffer reproach for a worthier cause, the Messiah himself." Remember, if Hebrews was written just prior to the revolt against Rome, this would have been a time of real pressure for greater harmony and unanimity, to stick with the system as is, to "not make waves." Differences could easily have resulted in great "reproach."

Does the phrase "outside the camp," then, imply leaving the Jewish system? Westcott makes an interesting observation but does not follow through on the implications.

> It is worthy of notice that the first tabernacle which Moses set up was "outside the camp" . . . The history is obscure, but as it stands it is significant in connection with the language of the Epistle.[61]

Moses did originally set up the tent or meeting "outside the camp" (Exod. 33:7) and spoke with God there, making it the earliest and "purest" form of established worship—from Essene eyes. The sacrifices originally took place here (cf. Heb. 13:11–12), making it the true center of the religious system, the place of communicating with God. Even later, it was the place for the cleansing ashes of the red heifer (Num. 19:9). The Yom Kippur sacrifice, "a sacrifice from which no one can eat" (cf. Heb. 13:10), was brought here to be consumed (Lev. 16:27). Yeshua died here, "outside the camp," the original place of worship and communication with God, in fulfillment of the sacrifice system and as the true center of Judaism.

The further reference to "outside the gate" would have struck another responsive chord among the Essenes. It would have coincided with their emphasis on the purity of the tabernacle and the impurity of the Temple—"outside the gate" indicating separateness from the "corrupted" (for the Essenes) Temple practices. So this command does not refer to withdrawing from the Jewish traditions and practices. Rather, it stands as a readily-understood challenge—in terms the Essenes would appreciate—to return to God and identify with true Judaism ("outside the camp and the gate") centered in Yeshua, apart from whom the whole thing is bereft of its ultimate meaning, life and reality.

The Essenes would also have responded favorably to Hebrews' emphasis on "the city to come" and not having a present "lasting city" (v. 14). They had gone "outside the gate," having left the city because of their objections to the corruptness of the priesthood and its operations, e.g. impurity of the practices, wrong calendar, etc. Therefore, they believed the Temple and city had to be cleansed before true worship could take place.[62] They viewed themselves as "exiles in the wilderness," awaiting entrance into a "new—and cleansed—promised land." So they had no present city; they looked for one to come. This would occur when Messiah ruled from Jerusalem. Verse 14 then repeats and reinforces the challenge of verse 13, using concepts and terminology familiar to the readers.

The background of the Near Eastern covenant procedures and the historical context of the Dead Sea community must affect our understanding of Hebrews. A biblical understanding of fulfillment must also shape our approach to the book. Finally, we must not push passages in Hebrews to contradict other Scriptures, such as Matthew 5:17–20, Romans 7:12ff., and the testimony of Acts to continued Jewish practice and identity. As these principles are kept in mind, the critical passages fall into place and the message of Hebrews becomes clear. Hebrews stresses identifying with Yeshua as the true center and intent of Judaism; it does not set aside Jewish identity and practice.

1. E.g. William Currie, "The Traditional Approach to Witnessing to Jews," Leland Crotts, "Response to The Messianic Jewish Approach": papers read at the Consultation on the Variations of Life and Expression of Jewish Believers, at Moody Bible Institute, Chicago, Illinois, Nov. 18–19, 1977.
2. Kenneth Kitchen, *Ancient Orient and Old Testament* (Chicago, Ill.: InterVarsity Press), p. 91.
3. Ibid., pp. 96–98, and Meredith Kline, *The Structure of Biblical Authority* (Eerdmans; Grand Rapids, 1972), pp. 115–117,120–122.
4. J. Barton Payne, *The Theology of the Older Testament* (Grand Rapids: Zondervan, 1971), p. 79.
5. Gerhard von Rad, *Old Testament Theology*, vol. 1 (New York: Harper and Row, 1962), p. 130.
6. Chester Lehman, *Biblical Theology*, vol. 1 (Scottsdale, PA: Herald Press, 1971), p. 122.
7. Cf. Johannes Pedersen, *Israel: Its Life and Culture*, vol. 1 (London: Oxford Univ. Press, 1946), pp. 308–309.
8. George Mendenhall, *The Tenth Generation: The Origins of the Biblical Tradition*, (Baltimore: John Hopkins Press, 1973), p. 15.
9. Ibid., p. 14.
10. Pedersen, pp. 191–193, 285–286.
11. Samuel Schultz, *The Prophets Speak* (New York: Harper & Row, 1968), pp. 46–47.
12. Samuel Schultz, session at the "Teach-In" sponsored by the Messianic Jewish Alliance of Chicago, Jan. 28, 1978.
13. E.W. Hengstenberg, *Christology of the Old Testament*, vol. 2, pp. 429–445, reprinted in *Classical Evangelical Essays in Old Testament Interpretation*, ed. Walter Kaiser (Grand Rapids: Baker, 1973), p. 238.
14. Cf. Schultz, pp. 38–39.
15. See, e.g. Frances Brown, S.R. Driver, and Charles Briggs, eds. *A Hebrew and English Lexicon of the Old Testament* (Oxford: Clarendon Press, 1966), p. 435.
16. Kline, pp. 118–119.
17. Hengstenberg, pp. 238, 239; Also cf. Schultz, pp. 38–39; Kline, pp. 118–119.
18. Oscar Cullman, *Salvation in History* (London: SCM, 1967), p. 263.
19. Cf. Walter Kaiser, "The Old Promise and the New Covenant," *Journal of the Evangelical Theological Society*, XV (1972), pp. 11–23.
20. Cf. George Peters, *The Theocratic Kingdom*, vol. 1 (Grand Rapids: Kregel, 1957), p. 322.
21. Quoted in Marten Woustra, "The Everlasting Covenant in Ezekiel 16:59–63," *Calvin Theological Journal* VI (1971), pp. 22–48.
22. Hengstenberg, p. 240.
23. Kaiser, pp. 16–17.
24. Wilber Wallis, "Irony in Jeremiah's Prophecy of a New Covenant," *Journal of the Evangelical Theological Society* XII (1969), p. 107.
25. Ibid., p. 109.
26. Ibid.
27. Hengstenberg, pp. 239–240, 243.

28. Ibid., p. 250.

29. Ibid., p. 245.

30. Kline, pp. 9–14,122.

31. Ibid., pp. 148–149.

32. Technically, under the dynastic succession understanding of the covenant, Yeshua was not the Messianic king until his resurrection, after the will and testament went into effect upon his death, hence the "Messianic secret." His ultimate succession to the throne awaits the Millennium, as 1 Cor. 15:23–26 and Luke 19:11–27.

33. Jakob Jocz, "The Old Testament as Commonground for Dialogue Between Church and Synagogue or Christians and Jews," *The Hebrew Christian*, XLVIII (1975), p. 186.

34. B.F. Westcott, *The Epistle to the Hebrews* (Grand Rapids: Eerdmans, 1970), pp. lviii, lxi.

35. Philip Goble, *Everything You Need to Grow* a *Messianic Synagogue* (Pasadena: William Carey Library, 1974), p. 10.

36. See *A Greek-English Lexicon of the New Testament and Other Early Christian Literature*, ed. W.F. Arndt and F.W. Gingrich (Chicago: University of Chicago Press, 1967), p. 415.

37. See Arndt and Gingrich on *pleroo*.

38. Cullmann, p. 33.

39. Willis Beecher, *The Prophets and the Promise* (Grand Rapids: Baker, 1963), pp. 365–386.

40. Richard Longenecker, *Biblical Exegesis in the Apostolic Period* (Grand Rapids: Eerdmans, 1975), p. 160.

41. Ibid., p. 160.

42. Yigael Yadin, "A Note on Melchizedek and Qumran," *Israeli Exploration Journal*, XV (1965) pp. 152–154; G.W. Buchanan, *To the Hebrews*, Anchor Bible series (Garden City, NY: Doubleday, 1972), pp. 99–100. Cf. also Longenecker, p. 161.

43. The abbreviations for the Dead Sea Scrolls and related material are as follows, 1QS—Manual of Discipline; 1QH—Psalms of Thanksgiving; 1QM—War Scroll; 11QMel—Melchizedek Scroll; CDC—Cairo-Damascus Covenant.

44. Yigael Yadin, "The Dead Sea Scrolls and the Epistle to the Hebrews," in *Aspects of the Dead Sea Scrolls*, ed. Chaim Rabin and Yigael Yadin (Jerusalem: Mapes Press, 1965), pp. 36–55.

45. Buchanan, p. 137.

46. Frank M. Cross, Jr., *The Ancient Library of Qumran* (London: Duckworth, 1958), p. 164.

47. Longenecker, p. 162. Cf. Alexander Nairne, *The Epistle to the Hebrews*, pp. lxxv–lxxvi. On the dating of Hebrews see John A.T. Robinson, *Redating the New Testament* (Philadelphia: Westminster Press, 1976), pp. 200–220.

48. Currie, "The Traditional Approach to Witnessing to the Jews," p. 9.

49. Westcott, p. 143.

50. F.F. Bruce, *Commentary on the Epistle to the Hebrews* (Grand Rapids: Eerdmans, 1970), p. 111.

51. Westcott, pp. 142, 143.

52. Buchanan, p. 137.

53. Ibid., pp. 137–138.

54. Cf. W.D. Davies, *Torah in the Messianic Age or the Age to Come* (Philadelphia: Society of Biblical Research, 1952).

55. Westcott, p. 252.

56. Bruce, p. 195.

57. Westcott, p. 254.

58. Bruce, p. 197.

59. Westcott, p. 254.

60. Matthew Black, *The Scrolls and Christian Origins* (New York: Thomas Nelson and Sons, 1961), p. 171.

61. Westcott, p. 442.

62. Buchanan, p. 235.

MESSIANIC JEWS AND THE TRI-UNITY OF GOD*

Michael Schiffman

Perhaps one of the most controversial issues between Jewish people and believers in the Messiah is the triune nature of God. Some have questioned why Messianic Jews, coming from a strong monotheistic heritage, would accept belief in a Tri-unity. It is assumed by some that Messianic Jews have accepted belief in the Messiah because of Gentile believers, and have consequentially accepted evangelical biblical theology because it came with the gospel message we received from the Gentiles. This is an error of understanding, and an over-simplification. Messianic Jews have accepted belief in the Messiah *in spite of* the Gentiles. It has been Gentile anti-Semitism over 18 centuries that has put a stumbling block between Jewish people and their Messiah.

Secondly, Messianic believers have not *inherited* anyone else's errors. This assumes that we do not think for ourselves, or are not capable of spiritual discernment. Messianic Jews have come to these conclusions and theological positions after examining the historical and biblical materials and concluding that they are correct. If what Messianic Jews believe coincides with evangelical theology, it is not because it has been inherited from evangelicals, but because the teaching is true.

Belief in the triune nature of God is not merely held by a group within the Messianic community, but is believed by every Messianic organization of the community: the Union of Messianic Jewish Congregations, the Fellowship of Messianic Congregations and the Messianic Jewish Alliance of America.

* This is a chapter from Michael Schiffman's *Return of the Remnant*. Baltimore: Lederer/Messianic Jewish Publishers, 1992.

A related area of difficulty for Messianic Jews is not the concept of the tri-unity, but the terminology. "Trinity" sounds very Catholic, and hence, very non-Jewish. "Tri-unity" is an attempt, but is not really much better. There may never be a suitable answer to the semantic issue because there will always be a tension between finding a word that is Jewishly palatable and one that is theologically precise. Of the two, accuracy is the most important, but palatability is also a concern.

Part of the problem in accepting this term lies in the fact that "Trinity" is a theological word, based on a biblical concept that bears no biblical nomenclature. If this were a biblical term, or if there were a Jewish equivalent, it would be more acceptable. Whether or not a word appears in Scripture, it should be considered acceptable as long as it accurately reflects the biblical data. The reason a formal trinitarian concept does not exist in the Old Testament is not because it is borrowed from Hellenism, as some suggest, but because as the revelation of God is progressive, so as with the nature of the Messiah himself, a full enough revelation did not exist in Jewish scripture until the New Covenant. The book of Hebrews tells us that "in these last days, God has spoken to us in His Son." Yeshua is the ultimate revelation of God, and through him we find the fullest revelation of God which we are capable of understanding.

Historically, the teaching of the Tri-unity was first articulated at the Nicaean council in 325 C.E., by the assembly of bishops, which was presided over by the Emperor Constantine. Constantine was an anti-Semite, as were a number of the bishops, so the conclusions of Nicaea were looked upon by some as having a distinctively anti-Jewish bias. It was at Nicaea that the Christian day of worship was formally changed to Sunday, and Christians were discouraged from celebrating Jewish Holy Days, in effect cutting Christianity from its Jewish roots. It was at Nicaea that Messianic Jews were challenged to turn away from their Jewish heritage and be Gentilized, or be branded as heretical and face the consequences of that label, which many did.

In spite of the negative factors surrounding Nicaea, it must be recognized that some good came out of it, and some truth was affirmed. Among the good that was accomplished was a clear affirmation of faith. The *Ekklesia* was facing serious theological challenges which forced it to examine its beliefs and define them in clear terms because of the heresies which needed to be answered. It was for this reason that the triune nature of God was delineated, not because of an anti-Jewish bias. It is not the anti-Semitic attitudes surrounding Nicaea that we affirm, but the truth that was articulated there, in spite of the anti-Semitism.

Another problem with the concept of the Tri-unity of God is the seeming antithesis it appears to be to the strict monotheism of Judaism. Some of the Trinity's opponents blame the Nicaean council's anti-Judaic bent for deriving a formula that would be unacceptable to Jewish people from the start. This concern is anachronistic because the concept of God's oneness had always been understood in broader terms than modern Judaism holds to-day. It could be reasonably argued that the Jewish understanding of God's oneness was interpreted more narrowly than in the past *in response* to the Christian understanding of God's oneness.

The fact is, the doctrine of the Trinity is not belief in three gods, but one God, who eternally exists in three persons, Father, Son, and Holy Spirit. Trinity is not a biblical term, but a theological one, seeking to accurately express all the data of Scripture relating to the nature of God. Some would say that the doctrine is not that important, as long as we believe Yeshua is the Messiah, because scripture teaches that "if you confess with your mouth, 'Yeshua is Lord' and believe in your heart that God raised Him from the dead, you will be saved." While this is true, it does not teach that if a person affirms the right labels he will be saved, but asks for the full acknowledgment of who God is, and if a person acknowledges a Messiah who is less than Scripture says he is, he is not affirming the Messiah of the Scriptures, and his confirmation is no confirmation. Affirming a Yeshua who is not God is not the same thing as affirming a Yeshua who is God, the creator of all things.

Some have no problem with the triune nature of God, but have a problem with the concept of persons in the Godhead. The reason for the term was not to express three independent, separate beings, but to guard against modalism, the idea that God is One, but takes on different forms, which would also indicate that God changes. Scripture, on the other hand, teaches that God never changes, but is the same yesterday, today, and forever.

Historically, the Nazarenes, the first-century Jewish believers who were biblically orthodox, were not the only sect which claimed to follow Yeshua of Nazareth. There were other groups who claimed to be Jewish and follow Yeshua as Messiah, yet their view of who he was fell far short of New Covenant teaching. It is important to understand that present-day Messianic Jews are the theological descendants of the Nazarenes and not of the heterodox groups that existed in ancient times. Yet, as they existed side by side, so too, in the twenty-first century, there are those who call themselves Messianic, yet their theology is not consistent with the Messianic mainstream. These groups and their beliefs will be briefly described below, followed by a discussion of Messianic understanding regarding the triune nature of God.

Irenaeus, who lived between 120–202 C.E., wrote concerning Cerinthus, a false teacher of the second century. He said,

> Cerinthus, again, a man who was educated in the wisdom of the Egyptians, taught that the world was not made by the primary God, but by a certain Power far separated from him . . . He represented Jesus as having not been born of a virgin, but as being the son of Joseph and Mary according to the ordinary course of human generation, while he nevertheless was more righteous, prudent, and wise than other men. Moreover, after his baptism, Christ descended upon him in the form of a dove from the Supreme Ruler, and that then he proclaimed the unknown Father, and performed miracles. But at last Christ departed from Jesus, and that then Jesus suffered and rose again, while Christ remained impassible, inasmuch as he was a spiritual being.[1]

Cerinthus' view of Yeshua may have been a *high view* in human terms, but it fell far short of the New Covenant teaching concerning the person of Yeshua, as well as the role of God as creator. It is difficult to explain why Cerinthus and his followers would have held such a low view of Yeshua, except that Irenaeus tells us that he was educated in the wisdom of the Egyptians. The New Covenant teachings of the nature of Yeshua and the Father may not have fit well into the educational grid of Egyptian teaching. The views of Cerinthus and his followers were considered too different from those of the mainstream believers in the New Covenant community of faith in the Messiah, and were consequently deemed to be outside the camp.

Closely related to Cerinthian teaching was the teaching of the Ebionites. Ebionites, in contradistinction to the Nazarenes, rejected the writings of Paul, claiming he was an apostate from the Law, and believed Yeshua was not divine. Origen, who lived between 185–254 C.E.. wrote concerning the Ebionites,

> Let it be admitted, moreover, that there are some who accept Jesus . . . and yet would regulate their lives, like the Jewish multitude, in accordance with the Jewish law, and these are the twofold sect of Ebionites, who neither acknowledge with us that Jesus was born of a virgin, or deny this, and maintain that He was begotten like other human beings.[2]

Origen was not unlike most Church leaders of his day who understood the theological distinction between Orthodox and heretical Jewish believers, yet lumped them together because of their Jewishness and similar lifestyles. This is as wrong as lumping Mormons and Evangelical Christians together because they both claim to follow Jesus, when the Jesus each follows is radically different from the other.

Those who call themselves Messianic, yet reject New Covenant teaching, cannot be rightly called Messianic, because Messianic Jews accept the Old and New Covenants as authoritative in all matters of faith and practice. The Yeshua these others follow is not the Yeshua of the New Covenant. The Yeshua of Messianic Judaism is fully man, yet fully God. He is the creator of all things, was incarnated and virgin-born, and has always existed. People may use Messianic terminology, worship like Messianic Jews, and be really nice people, but if the Yeshua they follow is less than the Yeshua we follow, we follow a different Messiah, and consequently we are not following the same God.

A group that was closely related to the Ebionites was the Elkesaites. According to the second-century historian Hippolytus, Elkesai taught that,

> . . . Christ was born a man in the same way that is
> common to all and that Christ was not for the first
> time on earth when born of a virgin, but that both
> previously and that frequently again he had been
> born, and would be born. Christ would thus appear
> and exist among us from time to time. . . .[3]

This group not only affirmed the virgin birth, but saw it as a
recurring event, yet denied the deity of Yeshua.

One final group, the followers of Sabellius, believed in One
God in three temporary manifestations. This is also called
modalism. According to Epiphanius,

> . . . a certain Sabellius came to the fore. Their doc-
> trine is, that Father, Son, and Holy Spirit are one
> and the same being, in the sense that three names
> are attached to one substance.[4]

All these groups claimed to be Jewish followers of Yeshua, but
their understandings of who Yeshua is differed greatly. Some had
problems with reconciling the oneness of God with the divinity of
Yeshua, while others had problems with issues of the Torah. These
are issues that Jewish believers struggle with today, and as God has
raised up the Messianic movement once again in these end days, so
too have the counterfeits also arisen, as in the beginning. The reason for discussing the issue of the triune nature of God is for the
same reason it has always been an important issue. Affirming faith
in Yeshua necessitates an understanding of who Yeshua really is.
Calling on the name of the Lord is not the chanting of a mantra,
but rather acknowledging the true nature of God. Calling on a
Yeshua who is not divine is calling into the wind. Calling on Yeshua, who is the divine Son of God, Lord of All, is salvation.

The Problem of Modalism

Modalism is a theological error common to many believers. It is
the simplest attempt to explain the triune nature of God while pre-
serving the oneness of God. This error is particularly appealing to
those who seek to affirm the oneness of God, which is foundational

to the Judaism of the Torah as well as to the teachings of the New Covenant. Concerning Modalism, eminent theologian Harold O.J. Brown has written:

> Modalism upholds the deity of Yeshua, but does not see Him as a distinct Person in regard to the Father. It holds that God reveals himself under different aspects or modes in different ages—as the Father in Creation and in the giving of the Law, as the Son in the Messiah Yeshua, and as the Holy Spirit after Messiah's ascension. Modalism stresses the full deity of the Messiah and . . . avoids the suggestion that he is a second God alongside the Father. Unfortunately, it abandons the diversity of Persons within the Godhead, and thus loses the important concept that the Messiah is our representative or advocate with the Father.
>
> Logically, modalism makes the events of redemptive history a kind of charade. Not being a distinct person, the Son cannot really represent us to the Father. Modalism must necessarily . . . teach that Messiah was human in appearance only; the alternative, on the basis of modalistic presuppositions, is that God himself died on the Cross. Since such an idea is considered absurd . . . the normal consequence is the conclusion that while the Messiah was fully God he only appeared to be man.[5]

The modalists emphasize the Gospel of John, with its statements stressing the oneness of Yeshua with the Father, for example, "I and my Father are One."

> . . . The word "one" in the Greek text of John 10:30 is the neuter *hen*, which suggests that the meaning is "one deity, one divine essence," rather than one Person. . . . If the Son is not a real person who can stand before the Father and address him, then the latter . . . concept of substitutionary sacrifice, which holds that Yeshua takes our place and

pays our debt to the Father, becomes at best a symbol and not a reality. Where modalism prevails, the concept of substitutionary satisfaction, or vicarious atonement, will necessarily be absent, and so modalism is sometimes adopted by those who object to the doctrine of vicarious atonement. More commonly, however, it simply arises as an attempt to reduce the mystery of the Trinity to a more understandable concept, even at the cost of the true humanity of Yeshua and the doctrine of substitutionary satisfaction.[6]

The problem we face is the problem all believers in Yeshua face. We seek to explain our faith, and, no matter what perspective we come from, we find ourselves trying to explain what is, in Scripture, a mystery. The answer for us may lie not in trying to explain that which has not been given to us to explain, but in affirming the truths of Scripture concerning God, and leaving further explanation as mystery. In other words, we affirm that God is one and eternally exists in three persons as Father, Son and Spirit of God, without seeking to explain how this can be. This position does not mean that the concept is illogical, only that it transcends our ability to comprehend the nature of God. It is presumptuous to assume that limited human beings can fully grasp the infinity of God. It is wisdom to acknowledge our limitations and affirm the truth we can grasp rather than seeking to explain things that go beyond our ability to comprehend. It is a far weaker position to attempt an explanation of that which we are unable to explain than to give an interpretation that falls short of biblical truth.

Some have pointed out that we need a different explanation of the triune nature of God because we present the message of Messiah to Jewish people, who find the Tri-unity to be conflicting with Judaism's monotheism. This is a fallacy. As Dr. Brown has said,

Orthodox trinitarian doctrine is summarized in the definition, "One essence [or nature, substance] in three Persons." There is but one God, as the Jewish *Shema* affirms (Deut. 6:4), for there is only one divine essence. This essence subsists in three distinct subjects or Persons. . . . The divine Persons are distinct, yet they cannot be separated from the godhead or from one another. It is apparent that human language is inadequate to do much more than to suggest the nature of the Trinity; it certainly cannot analyze it or explain it.[7]

The real issue believers in the Messiah must address to the Jewish people is the Messiahship of Yeshua. The doctrine of the Tri-unity is not an apologetic, but an explanation. People may object to its language, but the fact is that it does not teach the existence of three deities, but of one alone, and it is not inconsistent with the *Sh'ma* or any other concept of biblical Judaism. The idea of three persons in the Godhead is well within the concept of Jewish thought, as is taught by the Zohar.[8] Holding to belief in one God, eternally existing in three persons, is not polytheism, is not beyond the pale of Jewish thought, and most importantly, *is* the teaching of Scripture. By accepting the biblical belief, we are not diminished in our Jewishness, because Jewishness is our heritage. What we are believing is based on God's revelation in his Messiah. The traditional Jewish view of God is incomplete because it is without the revelation of God in the Messiah. The way to bring this message to our people is to share the Messiah, because he is the key to faith and understanding.

1. Irenaeus, *Against Heresies*, I 26, 1.
2. Origen, *Against Celsus*, V. 61.
3. Hippolytus, *The Refutation of All Heresies* IX.
4. Epiphanius, *Against Heresies*, LXII, I.
5. Harold O.J. Brown, *Heresies: The Image of Christ in the Mirror of Heresy and Orthodoxy from the Apostles to the Present*, (Grand Rapids: Baker Book House, 1984) p. 99.
6. Ibid., p. 100.
7. Brown, *Heresies*, p. 146.
8. Rabbi Tzvi Nassi. *The Great Mystery: How Can Three Be One?* (Cincinnati: Messianic Literature Outreach, 1990).

MESSIANIC JEWS AND ISRAEL

MESSIANIC JEWS AND THE LAW OF RETURN

Elliot Klayman

> Therefore, we conclude, as a matter of law, that a Jew who has not voluntarily left the Jewish community is a Jew according to *halakhah* and to the "man on the street" for purposes of the Law of Return. We further conclude that it is not for this court or for any civilized nation to interfere with one's right of thought, faith, or personal belief and that under the Law of Return one who was born Jewish does not cease to be Jewish regardless of his/her subjective convictions.

This is how we had hoped the Beresfords' decision would have played out. However, the Israeli High Court has taken another approach and in a unanimous decision has held that one who embraces Yeshua as Messiah is no longer Jewish for the purpose of the Law of Return. Unless there is a reversal of this decision, it is clear that the first century schism between Messianic Jews and the rest of the Jewish community is reconfirmed. And, unless the decision is reversed, Messianic Jews will have to reconsider their strategy for returning to the homeland.

Historical Overview

Israel, in the first century, was not made up of a homogeneous community but consisted of a variegated community. Some were Pharisees, who believed in the resurrection of the dead and the existence of angels; others were Sadducees, who opposed the Pharisees. The Herodians were the secular political ruling class, and they were probably devoid of a heartfelt religious conviction and practice. Then there were the Zealots, who were bent on overthrowing the Roman government and liberating the Jewish populace. The Essenes were a religious sect that rejected the priestly order as practiced in Jerusalem, and erected what they thought to be a purer priestly order. The Nazarenes followed Yeshua as the Messiah.

There was also a difference of opinion when it came to the Messiah. Some thought that the Messiah would establish his kingdom immediately on earth and overthrow the Roman rule. Others did not. Israel was then and is now a pluralistic community.

Within the first century, Jewry encompassed Messianic Jews, of whom there were many. We know that on the day of Shavu'ot (recorded in Acts 2) 3,000 came to believe in Yeshua, and were immersed. The next day 5,000 more were added to the Nazarenes, not counting the women and children; and the Lord added Jewish people to the ecclesia daily. Now we have a number of other accounts of priests, scribes, religious rulers, and members of the Sanhedrin who believed. Rav Sha'ul, a devout Jew, came to the Messiah. It is apparent that he, along with others, attended the Temple and the synagogues, and practiced the traditions and customs alongside unbelieving Jews.

In 67 C.E. the Romans besieged the city of Jerusalem and the Nazarenes fled to Pella instead of staying to fight. They were mindful of Yeshua's command to "flee when you see the armies surrounding Jerusalem." This flight, of course, did not endear them to the rest of the Jewish community, and they became suspect. Then, about 132 C.E. an attempt was made to liberate the city. At first the Messianic Jews, many of whom returned, joined in the fight, until Bar Kochba, the leader, was proclaimed the Messiah. Because of this proclamation, the Messianic Jews refused to support the liberation movement. They were *de facto* kicked out of the community and accounted as traitors (*m'shummadim*). Over a half-million Jews lost their lives in the Bar Kochba revolt, which eventually failed. Nonetheless, the schism between the Messianic Jews and the rest of the Jewish community deepened.

The Law of Return

The Law of Return is a secular Israeli law which gives every Jew who has not converted to another religion the right to return to the land as a new immigrant (*'oleh chadash*). The new immigrant is entitled to tax breaks and other benefits. The Law, passed by the Israeli Parliament in 1950, was derived from the Declaration of Statehood, which declared Israel as a homeland to the Jews who had been persecuted on the face of the earth. The Law also grants the right of return to spouses, children and grandchildren of Jews who have not voluntarily changed their religion. The phrases "converted to another religion" and "voluntarily changed religion" have been the subject of judicial interpretation.

The Case Law

The first decision relevant to Messianic Jews to come before the High Israeli Court was the Brother Daniel case. Brother Daniel was a Polish Jew who helped save Jews from Nazi persecution and genocide. While escaping from persecution himself, he wound up being sheltered in a Catholic convent, and ultimately converted to Catholicism. He wore monastic robes and a cross around his neck. After the war, he moved to Israel with the Carmelite Catholic order and sought citizenship under the Law of Return. The case rose to the High Court, and the court held that the "man on the street" would not account Brother Daniel a Jew, since he had converted to Catholicism. Although the case did not speak directly to Messianic Jews, it sounded a warning that those who were born of Jewish parents were not necessarily Jews for the purposes of the Law of Return. Clearly, here Brother Daniel had converted in lifestyle, culture and otherwise, to another religion.

The next case to arise involved a Gentile couple, the Hutchens, whose love of Israel prompted them to convert to Judaism. They then went to Israel and applied for citizenship under the Law of Return. However, they were challenged on the basis that their conversion was fraudulent since they believed in Yeshua as Messiah at the time of conversion. When word traveled back to the rabbinate in Chicago, the conversion was revoked. This made the High Court's task easy, holding that a conversion which is revoked according to the Law of *halakhah* is no conversion and hence the Hutchens were not Jewish; consequently, they did not qualify for return under the Law. The court made a gratuitous comment that "Judaism had spewed them out and they are allowed no entry into the Jewish community."

Esther Dorflinger was a Jewish believer in Yeshua who, according to the record in the High Court, had been baptized in a church in the United States and practiced Christianity. Her application for citizenship under the Law of Return was denied. The court applied a test to determine "conversion to another religion." It looked at whether the other religion claimed the person as one of theirs. After looking at Jewish sources to determine Christian doctrine and community the High Court acclaimed that Esther Dorflinger had converted to another religion because Christianity with one accord claimed her, since she believed in Yeshua and was baptized.

The scene was set for the case of the Beresfords, Messianic Jews from South Africa, who sought citizenship under the Law of Return. After a denial of their petition for citizenship the case rose to the High Court. The Beresfords kept *kashrut* (*kosher*), lived a culturally Jewish life, and were not members of a church but regularly attended a Messianic Jewish congregation. They had not been baptized into a church, but were ritually immersed in a *mikveh*. A three-judge High Court panel held unanimously that the Beresfords were not entitled to immigrate under the Law of Return because they had converted to another religion. One justice, Deputy President Menahem Elon, examined the case first under the perspective of the other religion and then under the *halakhic* perspective, and arrived at the same conclusion. He found, as had the court in *Dorflinger*, that Christianity accounts one as a member of its religion who has embraced Jesus as Divine. However, this judge went on to state his preference for determining whether a person had converted to another religion by examining Jewish law and sources. Under a *halakhic* and historical approach he found that Judaism has excluded from its community one who has named the name of Jesus as Messiah.

The second judge, Aron Barak, examined the case under the dynamic secular approach and arrived at the same conclusion as Justice Elon, although he rejected Elon's religious approach. He refused to determine who has "converted to another religion" from the perspective of the "other religion" or from that of Jewish religious law. Under Barak's dynamic secular approach he looked at the "consensus of opinion" and found that today Jews who believe in Jesus are held to have converted to another religion by the "man on the street." He left open the fact that under this approach time may change the result. The court rejected a poll conducted by the Israeli equivalent of the Gallup Poll which found that about 75% of the "men on the street" believe that Messianic Jews should be entitled to immigrate under the Law of Return.

Justice Halima, the third judge, without a written rationale, simply agreed with the outcome.

The Beresfords commenced a new case based upon Judge Barak's "dynamic liberal" test. They sought to position themselves under this test by dissociating themselves from activities that put them in the Messianic Jewish "camp," namely being a member of, and attending, a Messianic Jewish congregation, and engaging in street evangelism. However, the High Court in *Beresford II* once again refused entry to them under the Law of Return, and reaffirmed what had been said in *Beresford I*, thus strengthening the precedent that a Jew who believes in Jesus has "changed to another religion," and cannot become a citizen under the Law of Return.

Implications for Messianic Jews

The ruling in the Beresfords' case clearly confirms what happened 1900 years ago. The Jewish believers have been expelled from the *Yishuv* (Jewish community in Israel). The decision comes as no surprise in many circles. Yes, we were hopeful, but any hope in the Israeli High Court or in any human instrumentality is misplaced. God is our vindication, our justification. It is he who made Messianic Jews, and no man or ruling can alter that reality. There is where our comfort lies. Why should we expect that in the world we would have it easy when we are told the opposite in Scripture? We will be persecuted, despised and hated for Yeshua's name's sake. But be of good cheer. He has overcome the world and in him we are more than conquerors. What then is our response? Should the Beresford decision stand, it is not the end of the world for Messianic Jews. We ought to continue steadfast in prayer for our Jewish brethren, for they know not what they do.

There is an honest and ethical route home even in the face of the Beresford decision. The Law of Return is not the only route to citizenship in Israel. One may still apply to immigrate and become a citizen or a permanent resident by making full disclosure. What God ordains he will perform. And remember that God works things out for good—even in the face of impossible situations.

The Beresford decision will mark us. We will be distinct and separate from the *Yishuv*, even more so than we are presently. This will require us to draw closer in fellowship and in union. Through this love, one towards another, they will come to know that we are believers with hope and life. Our witness will not go unnoticed.

The Messianic Jewish community is growing in Israel from within and from without. The body of believers has always grown when it has been watered by persecution. Anti-missionary groups are growing to combat and warn of the phenomenon. They are spending increased amounts of money to repudiate the claims that we make about God and Messiah Yeshua.

Finally, we must believe God when he says that all things work together for good for those who love God and are called according to his purpose. We love our brethren and want so much to be a part of the community to which we belong. But God has called us to sacrifice for now and be "separated" for a season for a greater cause—the salvation of our Jewish people.

THE PEOPLE OF GOD, THE PROMISES OF GOD AND THE LAND OF ISRAEL

David H. Stern

God promises the Land of Israel to the Jews. This promise has not been revoked, and, like all of God's promises, it will be fulfilled through our blessed Messiah, Yeshua, Lord and Savior of all humankind—Jews, Arabs and everyone else. For in him all of God's promises are Yea and Amen (2 Cor. 1:20).

Mainstream Christianity has, in my view, gone through fantastic exercises, distorting vast areas of theology, in avoiding this obvious truth, stated by God century after century in the Hebrew Bible, which, together with the New Testament, constitutes God's exclusive inspired Word to humanity.

More specifically, these distortions have affected the theology of God's people (ecclesiology, "Israelology"), soteriology in its corporate aspects, the theology of the covenants, the theology of the *Torah* ("the Law"), the theology of God's promises, and, of course, the theology of the Land. Much of this has resulted from a mistaken effort, dating from at least the second century, to divorce the Church from the Jewish people—in contradiction to Eph. 2:11–12, which states that Gentile Christians have, through their faith in Yeshua, been "brought near" to the commonwealth of Israel.

To see what a correct Christian theology of the Land should be, we must try to correct the most egregious of these theological mistakes. For the theology of the Land is a relatively minor part of theology as a whole. Conclusions reached in these more important

* The original version of this article appeared in Fuller Theological Seminary's publication *Theology News and Notes,* Volume 41, Number 4, pp. 7–11, 23 (December 1994). A number of revisions, adaptations and additions have been made for the Theology of the Land Consultation in Droushia, Cyprus, June 27–July 2, 1996.

areas of theology determine the possibilities available for a theology of the Land. Mistakes in those areas will produce mistakes in the theology of the Land.

Mistakes in the Theology of the People of God

The people of God are a chosen people, a kingdom of priests, a holy nation, witnesses for God, a people with a mission, a people with a Book, and a blessing to the nations. The Bible applies such descriptions to both the Church and the Jewish people. Therefore any proper theology of God's people must take account of both Jews and Christians. Not only that, it must take account of Messianic Jews as being 100% Jewish and 100% New Testament believers.

The usual theologies of God's people, both Jewish and Christian, are too simple. Much of non-Messianic Jewish theology, of course, portrays the Jews as God's people and takes no account of the Church at all. The *Rambam* (Rabbi Mosheh Ben-Maimon, or "Maimonides," 1135–1204) and his followers broke new ground by concluding that Yeshua and Mohammed had brought many Gentiles to a true though imperfect faith in the God of Israel. Franz Rosenzweig (1886–1929) developed this into Two-Covenant Theology, which says that Christians are saved and come to the Father (John 14:6) through Yeshua and his New Covenant, but Jews don't need him or it because they are already with the Father through the Mosaic Covenant. (Some Christian theologians, e.g., Reinhold Niebuhr and Rosemary Reuther, in an attempt to honor Jewish sensibilities, especially since the Holocaust, have bought into Two-Covenant Theology and use it as an excuse not to evangelize Jews—in direct violation of the New Testament. But that is another issue.)

The simplest Christian theology of the people of God, Replacement Theology, says that the Church has not been "brought near" to the Jews but has *replaced* the Jews as God's people, the erroneous rationale often being that the Jews rejected Jesus and therefore lost the blessings promised them and receive only the curses. At best they are portrayed as just one of the nations, no longer having any special status with God. According to this theology the Jews have no longer any promise from God concerning the Land of Israel because they are no longer God's people. Unfortunately this anti-Semitic theology remains the most widespread in the Church, and efforts to patch it up or hide its anti-Semitic thrust fool no one except those who want to be fooled. (I have intentionally avoided the term Covenant Theology in this paragraph, because some versions of Covenant Theology do not espouse the replacement concept. However, many versions do.)

In the 19th century Dispensationalist Theology, attempting to present a more balanced and less anti-Jewish view, one that would see that the Jews have not become merely another nation, portrayed them as God's earthly people and the Christians as God's heavenly people. This strict separation of roles did not deal with the problem of Messianic Jews—do they ascend at the Rapture with the Church or remain below, loyal to their Jewish people? Either profoundly unsatisfying answer demonstrates the absurdity and inadequacy of this theological solution to the question of God's people.

Any right theology of the people of God must account not for one or two groups but three. Rom. 11:17–26, in the analogy of the olive tree, depicts natural cut-off branches (non-Messianic Jews), grafted-in wild branches (Gentile Christians) and formerly cut-off but now regrafted-in natural branches (Messianic Jews). I use the term "Olive Tree Theology" for any theology of the people of God which acknowledges that the Jews and the Church are each imperfect subpeoples of God, and that Messianic Jews belong to both. Without foreclosing on the eschatological possibilities, this theology must surely postulate that when all Israel is saved (Rom. 11:26), the two subpeoples will, at least in some senses, become one.

How did the Christian theologies of God's people miss this? The chief reason must be, as I suggested earlier, the tendency to disassociate the Church from its Jewish roots, an essentially anti-Semitic enterprise. But I can imagine another, more mundane explanation: I suppose theologians, like the rest of the human race, are lazy, and prefer not having to deal with all three groups at once if they can get by with a theory involving only one or two of them!

God has not rejected his people Israel (Rom. 11:1); he will not cast them off, at least not until the sun and moon cease to exist (Jer. 31:35–37). The immediately preceding verses (Jer. 31:31–34) are the very ones and the only ones that specifically hold out the promise of a "new covenant" with the house of Judah and the house of Israel. The authority of the New Testament itself depends on those verses. How then can one make void the next three verses, which make the people Israel and therefore the promise of the Land virtually eternal?

In conclusion, a right theology must clearly show that the Jews are still God's people—or, more accurately, along with the Church, one of God's two sub-peoples. If this is so, one must stop questioning *whether* God's promises to the Jews are still valid and instead ask how they apply in the present context. That means asking *how* God's promise that the Jews will have the Land of Israel as an everlasting possession is going to be, or is already being, fulfilled.

Mistakes in Corporate Aspects of Soteriology and in Understanding God's Promise

The individualistic Protestant Western world tends to stress the individual aspects of salvation. But the Bible, reflecting a Middle Eastern viewpoint that is still widely held today, gives equal weight to corporate aspects. One way in which this is done is by identifying the individual leading God's people with the people as a whole, as, for example, at 1 Kings 9:3–9, where God adjures King Solomon that his obedience or disobedience will determine Israel's future. Clearly the New Testament, written by Jews, continues this cultural pattern of identifying the king with his people in portraying Yeshua as the head of his Body, the Messianic Community (Church) (Eph. 1:22–23). Less well understood is the fact that Yeshua is also similarly identified with the Jewish people. This is expressed indirectly by Mattityahu (Matthew). At Matt. 2:15 he cites Hos. 11:1 ("Out of Egypt I called my son"), which the author considers "fulfilled" by Yeshua's return from Egypt to the Land of Israel. What is the fulfillment? Surely the verse in its context refers to the exodus of the Jewish people under Moses, and "my son" does not speak of Yeshua but alludes to Exod. 4:22, where the people of Israel are collectively called God's "son." By the novelty of referring Hos. 11:1 to Yeshua, Mattityahu hints at a deep truth, that Yeshua and his people Israel, the Jewish people, are intimately identified one with the other.

Yet while there are such things as deep truths, it will not do to say, as Replacement Theology does, that specific promises to the

Jewish people are somehow mystically "fulfilled in Yeshua" already; the deep truths of Scripture cannot violate its plain sense. The promise of the Land of Israel is forever, and the plain sense of this is that the Jewish people possess the Land (at least in trusteeship; see below, numbered paragraph 4) and live there. To say that the New Covenant transforms this plain sense into an assertion that those who believe in Yeshua come into some vague spiritual "possession" of a spiritual "territory" is intellectual sleight-of-hand aimed at denying, cancelling and reducing to nought a real promise given to real people in the real world! This is an intellectually unacceptable way of dealing with a text or with ideas.

Nevertheless, those who insist that all of God's promises to the Jews now apply willy-nilly to all believers in Yeshua, regardless of for whom they were intended, and not to the Jewish people (for whom they were in fact intended) must consider this: there are Jews who are believers. Why should not these constitute the present basis for God's continuing to consider the Jewish people the recipients of the promise of the Land? Why should the literal meaning of the promise be cancelled and replaced by its spiritual/ allegorical application to all believers? Why should this promise apply, in a literal sense, to Gentiles of any kind, whether believers or not? The Messianic Jews are the "righteous remnant" (Rom. 9:6–18) for whose sake God always extends himself—whether for ten in Sodom (Gen. 18:22–32) or for seven thousand in Elijah's day (Rom. 11:1–7). This is all the more so because the Messianic Jews are called the "firstfruits" of the Jewish people, with the stated necessary implication that "the whole lump," i.e., the Jewish people as a whole, "is holy" (Rom. 11:16). As if this were not enough, it is in this same section of Romans (chapters 9–11) that Sha'ul (Paul) reminds his readers that "the promises," which include the promise of the Land, belong to his "kinsmen according to the flesh" (Rom. 9:3–4). Finally, Isa. 51:10 says that "the redeemed of the Lord shall return and come with singing unto Zion, and everlasting joy shall be upon their head." If these "redeemed of the Lord" who have "come with singing unto Zion" are not the Messianic Jews now living in the Land, then who are they? In sum, even if there were not other reasons, God's promise of the Land to the Jewish people would remain literally valid today for the sake of the faithful remnant, the Messianic Jews.

It is common for Christians to suppose that the New Testament has little or nothing to say about the Land. In fact the New Testament refers no less than 18 times to the Land, although most New Testament translations conceal that fact. The Greek phrase *e ge* is usually translated "the earth," but in the New Testament it often refers to the Land of Israel. Two references are explicit—Matt. 2:20–21 calls the Holy Land "*Eretz-Israel*" ("the Land of Israel")—the New Testament never calls it Palestine. Four are citations from the *Tanakh*—Matt. 5:5 (Ps. 37:11, where the context, Yeshua addressing his Jewish disciples, requires the rendering, "the meek [i.e., Jewish believers] shall inherit the Land"); Matt. 24:30 and Rev. 1:7 (Zech. 12:10, 14, "all the [twelve Jewish] tribes of the Land shall mourn"), and Eph. 6:3 (Deut. 5:17, the "first commandment with promise... that you may live long in the Land"). Five are based on the *Tanakh* without being direct citations—Luke 4:25 and Ya'akov (James) 5:17, 18 (alluding to 1 Kings 17:1; 18:1, 45); Messianic Jews (Hebrews) 11:9 (alluding to Gen. 12; 13; 15; 20; 23); and Rev. 20:9 (alluding to Ezek. 38–39). The remaining eight are implied by the context (Matt. 5:13; 10:34; 27:45; Mark 15:33; Luke 12:51; 21:23; 23:44; and Rev. 11:10. Clearly the physical Land of Israel is not ignored in the New Testament.

Dispensationalists sometimes regard Romans 9–11 as a "parenthesis" in Sha'ul's argument, understood as moving directly from Chapter 8 to Chapter 12. This is an error in analysis. Chapters 9–11 form a crucial part of the thread of Sha'ul's thought in the Letter to the Romans. In Chapter 8 he brings his description of the process of individual salvation to its climax with a series of amazing promises culminating in the assertion that nothing can separate us believers from the love of God that comes through Yeshua the Messiah, our Lord.

"But," asks the Gentile Christian reader in Rome, "what about the Jews? God made them so many promises, yet they have not, as a people, accepted Yeshua's Messiahship. They have gotten off the track. How can God bless them with the fulfillment of these many promises if they turn away from the Messiah? And, more to the personal point, how can I, a Gentile Christian in Rome, trust God to fulfill these promises to me that you have told me about, if I can't see how God will fulfill these much older promises to the Jews?"

Sha'ul thus is obligated to talk about the Jewish people and God's promises to them. His answer is that while there is and always has been a believing remnant (in the present dispensation, the Messianic Jews), it will be through the ministry of the Gentiles to the Jews that all Israel (Israel's majority or Israel's establishment—not necessarily every single Jew) will be saved, and God will fulfill all his promises to them, for God's gifts and calling are irrevocable (Rom. 11:29)—and one should surely consider God's promise of the Land to the Jews a "gift," in the sense of this verse. Only now, after this reassurance that God remains faithful to his people the Jews and will fulfill his promises to them, promises which include permanent possession of the Land of Israel, can the non-Jewish Roman Christian be confident enough in God's promises to him to be able to pay attention to Sha'ul's instructions in Chapters 12–15.

Mistakes in the Theology of the Covenants and of the *Torah*

Space does not allow me to analyze in depth the errors found in Christian theologies of the covenants and of the *Torah*, but the above discussion hints at the directions I would take in addressing these aspects of Christian theology on which a correct theology of the Land of Israel depends.

Basically, there are two points I would make. First, I would follow Paul's argument in Gal. 3:15ff. that a later covenant cannot cancel an earlier one. He says that the Mosaic Covenant, made 430 years after the Abrahamic one, does not abolish the Abrahamic Covenant and its promises. Likewise, I would argue that the New Covenant does not abolish either the Abrahamic or the Mosaic Covenant, both of which contain promises concerning the Land. Nor would the New Covenant abolish prophecies made long after Moses died by the prophets of Israel, up through and including such prophets as Zechariah, who lived after the Babylonian Exile and still promised a return of the Jews to the Land—which proves that the post-Babylon return did not exhaust or entirely fulfill these promises.

Second, I would take note of the fact that the promises and laws of these covenants and of the *Torah* do not all apply to everyone. For example, the *Torah* requires the king of Israel to write a *Torah* scroll and read it. This law applies to only one person in all of Israel—no one else has to write a *Torah* scroll. If, as I believe, *Torah* still applies today (and, by my understanding of Heb. 8:6

the New Testament itself has been made *Torah*), one should not suppose that every believer is required to write a *Torah* scroll. This is a law that applies not to all Israel, or all leaders or all priests (*cohanim*), but only to the king. Similarly, there are many laws and promises in the *Torah* which apply to the Jewish people but are not transferred to all believers. My analysis of Gal. 2:11–21 shows that while the Jewish dietary laws (*kashrut*) are *not* abolished by Yeshua or Paul, their application in certain situations is modified; in particular, in the situation in Galatia where Jewish believers were withdrawing from table fellowship with Gentile believers, Paul renders a legal decision (a *din Torah*, a determination of *halakhah*) that the New Covenant principle that believers should be in fellowship with each other (1 John 1:1–4) takes precedence over the laws for keeping kosher, so that if the two conflict, a Messianic Jew must give up *kashrut* to preserve fellowship in the Lord. But one will not find that the promise of the Land has to be given up or compromised, although the manner in which believers may pursue this promise has to be constrained by any New Covenant spiritual principles that are applicable. For more on this, see below.

A Messianic Jewish Biblical Theology of the Land

While Christian theology as it stands does not provide a theological environment suited to expressing a correct theology of the Land of Israel, one Messianic Jewish scholar here in Israel has forged ahead and developed aspects of such a theology. Joseph Shulam is Provost of the Messianic *Midrashah* (Seminary), elder of *Kehilat Ro'eh Israel* ("Shepherd of Israel" Congregation), and leader of the Netivyah Organization for Bible Research, under whose auspices he and a colleague have written a substantial commentary on Romans. In studying the Land in the light of the Bible and Jewish commentators he makes the following points:

1. Why does the *Torah* (the Pentateuch) start with the story of the creation of the world? *RaShI* (Rabbi Shlomo Yitzchaki, 1040–1105) answers: "In case the nations would say to Israel, 'You are bandits because you conquered and destroyed the land of the seven Canaanite nations,' Israel can respond by saying, 'The whole earth is the Lord's; he created it all, and he gave it

to whom he pleased. By his will he gave it to them, and by his will he took it from them.'" In other words, the Jewish claim to the Land of Israel is neither political nor ideological but based and completely dependent on God's sovereign decision to promise, give or withhold.

2. The borders of the Promised Land are sometimes not stated (Gen. 12:3ff.; 13:15–17), sometimes stated generally (Exod. 23:31, "from the Reed [Red] Sea to the Sea of the Philistines, and from the Desert to the River"; Deut. 34:1 and Judg. 20:1, "from Dan to Be'er-shcva"), and sometimes very specifically (the description of the tribal borders in the book of Joshua).

3. The promise is forever (Gen. 24:5, 7, no time limit; Gen. 48:4; Lev. 25:4; Josh. 14:9, "an everlasting posession"; Ps. 105:7–11, "a thousand generations," which, literally, by biblical standards, is 40,000 years).

3. However, God can not only bring his people into the Land of Promise, their eternal possession, at his will, but he can and does remove them at his will (see point #1 above). He does the latter in response to their disobedience (Exodus 28), but he returns them by his grace (Ezekiel 36, Jeremiah 31). Thus eternal possession does not imply continuous habitation; rather, a trusteeship model is more appropriate.

4. Although some Jewish settlers cite the book of Joshua as authority for "conquering" Palestinian-occupied land, this is an illegitimate use of Scripture. Joshua had a clear and direct commandment from God both to conquer and to kill the inhabitants of the seven Canaanite nations. It was a very specific *ad hoc* commandment, and it did not extend to all living in the Land, only to certain nations that had had 400 years in which to repent of their evil ways (Genesis 15). It cannot be stated rationally that the Palestinian Arabs today are in the category of the Canaanites in the days of Joshua son of Nun. Such an ethnic comparison expresses an unbiblical attitude of racism, nationalism and hate which cannot be disguised by calling it "faithfulness to God's promises." Moreover, the prophetic vision of resettlement of the Land after the exile is not based on violent takeover but on divine intervention (Isaiah 60–61, Ezekiel 36–37).

5. The process of settlement was not an act of brute force; God prepared the way (Exod. 23:28, "I will send the hornet before you"; likewise Josh. 24:12). Also it was gradual; Canaanites

remained in the Land till the days of Solomon, living in coexistence (1 Kings 9:11–13).

6. The patriarchs received the promise of the Land but waited patiently for God to fulfill it and died without seeing that fulfillment (Hebrews 11). They did not use force to displace the inhabitants. Abraham related civilly to them, paying full price for the Cave of Machpelah (Genesis 23). See also Num. 14:40–45; 21:1; 33:40; Deut. 1:41–44.

7. There is no relationship whatever between the Philistines of biblical times and the Palestinians of today, even though the names are related. The Philistines were descended from Japheth, while the Palestinians are Arabs descended from Shem.

8. Solomon gave Hiram twenty cities in Galilee (1 Kings 9:10–13). He gave away land. If he had believed that the Land of God's promise had innate holiness, he would not have turned over twenty cities to Hiram for the wood Hiram supplied to build the Temple. And if land can be given in payment for wood, how much more can land be given for peace!

So far as I know, among Messianic Jews Shulam's work is *sui generis.* But in the modern development of Land theology, non-Messianic Jews have understandably led the way. Two such pioneers were Avraham Kook, Israel's first Chief Rabbi, and his son Rabbi Zvi Yehuda Kook, whose views are summarized in his book *Torat Eretz Yisrael* ("Doctrine of the Land of Israel"), published in English by Torat Eretz Yisrael Publications (20-Gimel Ben-Zion, Jerusalem). These two inspired thousands of religious Jews to settle in the Territories after 1967.

The Peace Process As Seen By Messianic Jews in Israel

Until now I have been presenting the theological underpinnings of the statement which opened this essay and which I can now take as axiomatic, that God's promise of the Land of Israel to the Jewish people is still in force—not canceled, not mystically fulfilled in Yeshua already or otherwise spiritualized at the expense of its literal meaning, and not transferred to or taken over by the Church.

Next, I want to examine what this promise means in relation to the ongoing peace process between the State of Israel, on the one hand, and the Palestinians and the Arab states, on the other—as three Israeli Messianic Jews see it. [Note: These three opinions were offered in late 1994; by now they are in some respects quite dated. However, I am presenting them anyway because one can still sense, behind their statements about the peace process at that time, their underlying theological positions.]

Let's look first at basic data concerning the Body of the Messiah in Israel. In my book *Messianic Jewish Manifesto* I estimated in 1988 that there were between 1,000 and 3,000 Jewish believers in Yeshua in the Land. This was before the big Russian *'aliyah* (immigration) that added a million Jews to the population of the State, including many thousands of Messianic Jews. It also was before Operation Shlomo brought 15,000 Jews from Ethiopia, of whom hundreds if not thousands are believers in Yeshua. I would therefore guess there are now between 3,000 and 10,000 Messianic Jews in Israel—which is still a tiny minority, less than one in five hundred, at most. There are some 50–100 congregations, the majority of which conduct their services in Hebrew, with others using English or Russian. Some meet in private homes, but most have regular meeting-places. Officially there are some 170,000 Christians, most of whom are Arabs affiliated with Eastern Orthodox or Catholic denominations.

Of the Arab Protestants, very few espouse the theology of the Land presented above. Where this is not due to ignorance or mistaken teaching, it can only be the result either of finding that theology at odds with political ambitions or of fearing the consequences of holding an unpopular view. I am always impressed with the courage of the occasional Arab Christian brother willing to admit that God has given the Land to the Jews as an eternal possession— a view which for him is very politically incorrect.

I asked several Messianic Jewish leaders here in Israel what was their opinion of the peace process. Reuben Berger, an elder of *Kehillat HaMashiach* (Congregation of the Messiah) in Jerusalem, answered as follows:

> The government has gotten itself into an enormous deception because of its unbelief in God and in the Bible, its willingness to sacrifice God-given Jewish identity to join the new world order, and its self-delusion concerning Arafat and Assad, whose goal remains the destruction of the State of Israel. In a

meeting Arafat thought was private he alluded to Mohammed's breaking a treaty with the Koresh tribe, implying he would do the same with the Oslo Accord. Why doesn't our government see this? God will never give Israel peace till the Jewish people know Jesus. About this I am optimistic, for we've seen slow steady growth in recent years, both numerically and spiritually. Since the peace process began more Israelis are getting saved. But the Gospel must go out to the Arabs too, and this work is close to my heart.

He also added these remarks about the Arab Christians:

There's a problem of division among them, and emigration. There's discouragement because of the problem with Islam, since Muslims greatly outnumber Christians in Israel and the Territories. Many in the Territories expect a decrease in rights for Christians. Jordan, when it was in control, allowed only mainstream churches to exist.

David Tel-Tsur is a high-school science teacher and an elder of *Kehilat Heftzibah* in Ma'aley-Adumim, a town east of Jerusalem, in the Territories. In response to my questions he wrote,

This is not a real peace! This is a false peace, the peace of men who deny the God of Israel (Ezek. 13:16). This is a peace implemented by "false prophets" (Jer. 6:14; 8:11, 15; 14:13–15; Ezek. 14:9–11), who refer to the "new Middle East." This peace stands against what God has said (Exod. 23:32). The words of the prophet Isaiah are very clear about this current process: Isa. 28:14–15. Our Lord said, "I didn't come to bring peace to the earth . . ."

There will be peace only when the Prince of Peace comes after destroying all His enemies and the enemies of Israel. [Before a man can engineer peace he must first himself] have peace with God.

Only then is peace between men possible. God doesn't need these sinners to bring His peace to the earth; this he will do only through his Son.

This is true also concerning Arafat. . . . Rabin shook this man's hand, a hand covered with Jewish blood. . . . The words of Exod. 17:14, 16 and Deut. 25:19 are clear with regard to the enemies of Israel.

This is a false peace [because the Muslim Arabs base it] on the Koranic principle of making peace with enemies: "If you cannot overcome your enemy once or twice, then make peace with him, and after a while destroy him." This "peace" is implemented only for the purpose of destroying Israel and the House of the Messiah Yeshua. The real Prince of Peace will come soon.

Shalom in the name of Yeshua.

Elhanan Ben-Avraham is a Messianic Jewish artist and writer in Jerusalem. He has written an article from which I have excerpted the following:

The idea of achieving "peace for a piece" (of land) is a delusion. Land is not the missing piece for peace. Two powerful currents, the Judeo-Christian ethic and Islam, that diverged for centuries, are meeting head-on. According to the Islamic vision, land once conquered by Islam must always remain in the possession of Muslims, not Jews—and above all, Jerusalem. Or, as former mayor Teddy Kollek, a Labor Party member, put it, ". . . in truth the Arabs have not yet given up on someday ruling Spain again. They will continue for generations, no matter how well we behave toward them, to see in us a people who have conquered their holy soils" (*The Jerusalem Post*, October 21, 1994).

The prophets of the Bible address the issue of Jerusalem. Zechariah describes a day when this city will become a burdensome stone and a cup of poison to the surrounding nations (chapter 12), and all the nations will be gathered by God against her in war (chapter 14). The prophet Joel (chapter 4) describes a specific day when God will have gathered the dispersed of Judah and Jerusalem, and says he will also gather all nations to the Valley of Yehoshafat ("the Lord has judged") to deal with them as they have dealt with Israel, in that they have *divided His land*. There is no doubt about the intention of the current Arab political move: to divide the Land of Israel into two states. That would leave Israel a narrow, difficult-to-defend mini-state. The area termed the "West Bank," that is, Judea and Samaria, the territory the Palestians intend for their state, is actually the Promised Land granted throughout the biblical account by God to the Jewish people.

Having lived in Israel now for 15 years, I personally see the good intentions of many individuals on both sides—which underscores the reality of the words, "Our struggle is not against flesh and blood, but against the rulers, against the powers, against the world forces of this darkness, against the spiritual forces of wickedness in heavenly places" (Eph. 6:12). I am certain that *shalom* will come. And it is clearly our obligation as servants of God to diligently seek it. But *shalom* is from above, from the One whose gift it is to give. This is the vision of all Israel's prophets.

Still, the peace process may bring us a measure of quiet here in the Middle East. If such quiet, perhaps even prosperity, comes, let us nevertheless take to heart Yeshua's warning that his return will resemble the days of Noah (Matt. 24:37), when the earth was filled with "violence" (Gen. 6:11, 13). In those verses the Hebrew word for "violence" is *hamas*. In our day one of Israel's most implacable enemies calls itself Hamas. So let us follow Yeshua's advice, to "watch vigilantly" (Matt. 24:42). But let

us also be like Noah in his generation, declaring the
good news of salvation and of the *shalom* proclaimed in God's covenant made through Yeshua
the Messiah here in Jerusalem.

Although these three are expressing only their own views, I
think I have the mind of Israel's Messianic Jewish community if I say
that few of us put much faith in the peace process. The first and most
obvious reason is one we share with nonbelievers: the level of terrorism remains high and shows no sign of diminishing. But even if it did
abate, we would question the process for two additional reasons aris-
ing out of our faith. First, many of us interpret biblical prophecies to
be telling us that peace simply is not to be expected; it is not what
God will be doing in the time prior to Yeshua's return. Second, as
believers we have a high standard for what peace ought to be. It is
not merely a ceasefire, or the exchange of ambassadors, or a multina-
tional force patrolling the borders to prevent terrorist infiltration.
Rather, it involves both individual peace with God and the setting up
of God's kingdom on earth. Neither of these will be accomplished
by any of the present leaders of the Middle East, or their successors.
Only Yeshua will restore the kingdom to Israel (as affirmed by Acts
1:6–7) and bring peace to the world.

Along these lines, holding to the Lord's standards of what
peace must entail, a number of Messianic Jews here apply Jer.
12:14–17, *mutatis mutandis,* to the situation in the Land: "Thus
says the Lord concerning all my evil neighbors who touch the heritage which I have given my people Israel to inherit: "Behold, I will
pluck them up from their land, and I will pluck up the house of
Judah from among them. And after I have plucked them up, I will
again have compassion on them, and I will bring them again each
to his heritage and each to his land. And it shall come to pass, if
they will diligently learn the ways of my people, to swear by my
name, 'As the Lord lives,' even as they taught my people to swear
by the Ba'al, then they shall be built up in the midst of my people.
But if any nation will not listen, then I will utterly pluck it up and
destroy it, says the Lord." In other words, peace in the Land depends on both Jews and Arabs being born again from above
through faith in Yeshua, the Messiah of Jews and Arabs alike.

Final Word: A Warning to Christians

In this I think I can safely claim to be speaking for virtually all Messianic Jews in Israel. Zechariah 12 and 14 proclaim a day when all nations will come against Jerusalem, and the Lord (that is, the Messiah Yeshua) will fight and defeat them. The Jewish people will be saved as they recognize and mourn for their Messiah, "whom they pierced." He, the Messiah, will be standing on the Mount of Olives, "with all his holy ones," repelling and defeating all the nations battling the Jews.

And where will you be? Will you be opposing the Jewish people as they defend their Land? Or standing with Yeshua? There seems to be no other option.

THE SIGNIFICANCE OF JERUSALEM FOR MESSIANIC JEWS

David H. Stern

I

To start with, Messianic Jews believe that the Bible is inspired by God. Therefore we accept what the Bible has to say about Jerusalem as God's truth for all humanity, since whatever it says about anything is true. The Bible says that the Land of Israel is where God will establish the Jewish people, and that Jerusalem is its capital city. Only the Christian Church's anti-Jewish "replacement theology"—which asserts that the Church has replaced the Jews as God's people, and therefore that God's promises to the Jews must be understood "spiritually" as being fulfilled to the Church and not to the Jews—has blinded the eyes of many Christians and others to this obvious biblical truth.[1]

According to the *Tanakh*, Melchizedek was from Salem, sometimes understood as being Jerusalem. Abraham brought Isaac to Mount Moriah, one of the four hills on which Jerusalem was built, to sacrifice him. David chose Jerusalem as the seat of his kingdom 3,000 years ago. The Temple was built in Jerusalem, and God dwelt in it. Judean kings ruled from Jerusalem for four hundred years. The Psalmist called Jerusalem "the City of God" and "the joy of the whole earth" (Ps. 46:4; 48:2). Frequently Jerusalem is called "Zion," for example, in the parallel phrases of Isa. 62:1: "For Zion's sake I will not hold my peace, and for Jerusalem's sake I will not rest." The Bible's "Zionism"—actually "Jerusalemism"—is described a few verses later: "Ye that make mention of the LORD, keep not silence, and give him no rest, till he establish, and till he make Jerusalem a praise in the earth" (Isa. 62:6–7). Prophets prophesied in Jerusalem. Among the prophecies: Jerusalem will be the millennial capital (Jer. 31:40; 33:16; Zech. 8:4–5; 14:20–21), with a

Temple for praise and thanksgiving sacrifices (Ezek. 43:20–21). And—of great interest to Messianic Jews—God's *Torah*, his teaching, will go forth from Jerusalem (Isa. 2:3; Mic. 4:1–4). But Zechariah prophesies that these events will provoke massive opposition from "all the people of the earth," with the consequence that God "will seek to destroy all the nations that come against Jerusalem" (Zech. 12:2–9). The prophet Joel put it like this: "When I restore the fortunes of Judah and Jerusalem, . . . I will enter into judgment with [all the nations] . . . on account of my people and my heritage Israel, because they have scattered them among the nations, and have divided up my land" (Joel 4:1–2 in Jewish versions or 3:1–2 in Christian versions).

According to the New Testament, Jerusalem was the locus and focus of Yeshua the Messiah's activity, especially his salvific activity, from babyhood through resurrection. He himself was and is the quintessential Jew. The *sh'lichim* (apostles) were Jewish, and, according to the book of Acts, their activity was largely centered in and flowed forth from Jerusalem. The "Messianic community" or "Church" began in Jerusalem, when God filled the disciples with the *Ruach HaKodesh* (Holy Spirit) on *Shavu'ot* (the Feast of Weeks, also called Pentecost). The Bible commands Jews to celebrate this holiday—likewise *Pesach* (the Feast of Passover) and *Sukkot* (the Feast of Booths)—in Jerusalem. The most important "Church council" in history took place in Jerusalem (Acts 15:1–29), where it was decided that Gentiles did not have to convert to Judaism in order to honor Yeshua and be "brought near" to the Jews, the people of God (Eph. 2:11–12). By the time of Acts 21:20 the number of Messianic Jews in Jerusalem had reached the "tens of thousands" (Greek *myriades*). Sha'ul (Paul), although his ministry was to Gentiles, remained a Jew all his life, indeed remained a Pharisee (Acts 23:6), and declared he had done nothing against the *Torah* (Acts 25:8). From Ephesus he hurried to get to Jerusalem in time to celebrate *Shavu'ot* (Acts 20:16).

In the New Testament, Jerusalem figures significantly in prophecy. Yeshua the Messiah prophesied the destruction of the Temple (Luke 21:6), which took place in the year 70 c.e. He also gave a prophecy that Jerusalem would be "trodden down of the Gentiles until the times of the Gentiles be fulfilled" (Luke 21:24). Many understand this to have occurred in 1967, when the Old

City of Jerusalem came under Jewish rule for the first time in 1,897 years. After his resurrection from the dead, Yeshua went into heaven from the Mount of Olives, just outside Jerusalem; the disciples were told that he would return "in the same way," which seems to mean to the same place. Jewish tradition, too, basing itself in part on Zech. 14:4, expects the Messiah to appear on the Mount of Olives.

The New Testament also makes considerable use of Jerusalem as a symbol. In Matt. 2:3; 3:5; and 23:37, Jerusalem represents the Jewish people generally. Luke intimates Jerusalem's central significance for Jews (Luke 13:33) and, derivatively, for the Gospel itself (Luke 24:47, Acts 1:8). The famous allegory of Gal. 4:25–26 makes earthly Jerusalem stand for the unsaved portion of the Jewish people, while the Jerusalem from above "is free," as is the Messianic Community of Jews and Gentiles united by faith in the Messiah Yeshua (compare the "heavenly Jerusalem" of Heb. 12:22).

II

But Messianic Judaism's background is not only biblical; our ideology has other sources, two of which are historical Judaism and historical Christianity. While neither is authoritative for our faith and practice, it cannot be denied that spiritually and culturally we have roots in both.

To begin with, we cherish Jerusalem just as do the rest of the Jewish people. As Ps. 137:5–6 puts it, "If I forget thee, O Jerusalem, let my right hand forget her cunning. If I do not remember thee, let my tongue cleave to the roof of my mouth; if I prefer not Jerusalem above my chief joy." Jerusalem has significance for all Jews, and on this point Messianic Judaism identifies with non-Messianic Judaism.

Here are two examples of this intimate longing for and relationship with Jerusalem. First is the phrase recited for centuries by Jews all over the world at the end of the *Haggadah*, the service for Passover: "Next year in Jerusalem!" Second is the most important prayer in Judaism, the *'Amidah* or *Sh'moneh-'Esreh*, which observant Jews pray in synagogues everywhere three times daily; it includes these lines:

> Sound the great *shofar* [ram's horn] for our free-
> dom, raise the banner to gather our exiles, and
> gather us together from the four corners of the
> earth [implied: to the Land of Israel]. Blessed are
> you, LORD, who gathers in the dispersed of his
> people Israel. . . . To Jerusalem, your City, may you
> return in mercy and dwell within it, as you have
> spoken. Rebuild it soon, in our days, as an eternal
> structure. Quickly establish within it the throne of
> David [on which the Messiah will sit]. Blessed are
> you, LORD, the Builder of Jerusalem. . . . LORD, our
> God, favor your people Israel and their prayer by
> restoring the service to the Holy of Holies in Your
> Temple. . . . May our eyes see your return to Zion
> [understood as meaning Jerusalem, as in Zech.
> 8:1–8] in mercy. Blessed are you, LORD, who re-
> stores his manifest Presence to Zion.

Although Reform Judaism has deleted aspects of these prayers, Orthodox and Conservative Judaism retain them all. Messianic Judaism
judges by the Scriptures any Jewish practices not specifically authorized or described in them. In this case, the Scriptures clearly promise the return of the Jewish people to the Land of Israel, with
Jerusalem as the capital city which is to have, at least at some point, a
rebuilt Temple, and from which the Messiah Yeshua, the Son of
David, will rule as King over the Jews and over the other nations.
Thus Messianic Jews can pray these non-Messianic Jewish prayers
and disagree with Christian theologies advocating a spiritualization
of the promises God made to the Jewish people about these matters.

This last remark introduces the subject of how Messianic Judaism relates to what Christianity has to say about Jerusalem. Apart
from the monastic movement in the Byzantine period and the Crusades, the Church has had little attachment to the Land of Israel or
to Jerusalem as a place to live and work, although pilgrimages to
visit Jerusalem are a part of Christian tradition and practice. Most
Christian references to Jerusalem have been to its history as the
place where Yeshua walked, ministered, died and rose again or to
its figurative, allegorical and prophetic meanings. Christians do not
proclaim for their lives an ongoing role for earthly Jerusalem.

While Roman Catholicism considers the first fifteen Messianic Jewish leaders of the Church in Jerusalem, up to the expulsion of all Jews in 135 C.E., to be its first fifteen popes, and while many Christian denominations have over the centuries obtained property and erected churches in Jerusalem and at other sites of Christian significance in Israel, there are no Christian prayers comparable to the Jewish ones cited above.

Nevertheless, Messianic Judaism can accept these figurative layers of significance for Jerusalem which Christianity sees in the New Testament and non-Messianic Judaism does not accept. They enrich Messianic Jewish celebration of the Jewish festivals (actually, better to call them the biblical festivals), which are biblically and traditionally centered on Jerusalem. Yeshua himself celebrated them there. Thus Messianic Jews cherish Jerusalem just as Christians do—as the city where Yeshua and his early Jewish followers lived, where the Messiah will return to rule, and as symbolic of all that our faith stands for.

III

But for Messianic Jews there are significances to Jerusalem which are in addition to those we share with Jews and with Christians. Because the Messianic community began in Jerusalem and spread from there, there is for those of us Messianic Jews who at present live in Jerusalem, first, a sense of identity and continuity with the Messianic Jews of the first century, and then, in consequence, an awesome sense of responsibility and excitement as we attempt to bring Yeshua back home to Jerusalem and to his Jewish people (in contrast with Christian missions that often extract Jews from their Jewish culture and religious background and bring them to a non-Jewish Jesus for whom the real Jerusalem has little valence). Our goal is nothing less than to re-establish, *mutatis mutandis*, the first-century Jerusalem Messianic Jewish Community as a model, guide and light both to the nations and to the Jewish people, so that the *Torah*, understood in the light of Messiah Yeshua's having come, will, as promised, go forth from Jerusalem. We are trying, on the one hand, to recreate and restore for the Church the Jewish context of Messianic faith and, on the other, to Messianize Judaism by renewing its wineskins (Matt. 9:17).

Jerusalem was the center of the worldwide Messianic community at least until 135 C.E and ruled by 15 Jewish "popes." But in
that year the Roman emperor Hadrian excluded all Jews, Messianic
and otherwise, from Jerusalem, and the Jerusalem Church became
Gentile. In that same period non-Messianic Jews too began treating Messianic Jews as pariahs (the Hebrew term *m'shummad*, used
today to refer to a Jew who accepts Yeshua, means "destroyed
one"). The return of non-Messianic Jews to Israel and Jerusalem is
well documented and widely known, but the return of the Messianic Jews is not. Joseph Wolff, a well-known Messianic Jew, came
to Jerusalem in 1822, and in 1841 Rabbi Michael Solomon
Alexander was delegated by the Anglican Church and the German
Lutherans to be the first modern "bishop of Jerusalem." A substantial portion of the subsequent history of Messianic Jews in Israel has been documented in a doctoral dissertation done at
Hebrew University by Gershon Nerel, Israel Secretary for the International Messianic Jewish Alliance.[2]

At present there are in Jerusalem at least several hundred Messianic Jews, and possibly more than a thousand, worshipping in
some ten congregations and contributing to the life of the city. (In
Israel as a whole, there are 3,000–10,000 Messianic Jews and 50–
100 congregations. The exact number is not easily determined,
since many Russian and Ethiopian immigrants and a few Orthodox
Jews believe in Yeshua but conceal their faith.) Most of this growth
in the Messianic Jewish population has taken place since 1967, the
year when, because of the Six-Day War, Jerusalem became a united
city under Israeli control.

Joseph Shulam, a Messianic Jewish congregational leader in
Jerusalem, has expressed some of the above ideas. He notes that
although the gospel is universal, it cannot be divorced from its
time, its geographical location, and the people among whom it was
acted out, the Jews.

> Take the gospel out of Jerusalem and plant it in
> Rome or somewhere else, or nowhere at all, and
> you make it into a Hellenistic pagan myth. Only
> Jerusalem brings the gospel back to its real and
> earthly, as well as its cosmic, dimensions. Jerusalem
> is the only city of which it can be said, "God dwelt

in this place." God's house was here for a thousand years. In the end the plan of salvation returns to Jerusalem. No one can escape that Jerusalem figures uniquely in salvation. So the gospel must return to Jerusalem, just as it came out of Jerusalem. Jerusalem must be related to not as an historical curiosity or an irrelevant accident in the salvation plan, but as a real place where Messianic Jews today are trying to rebuild the hope of Israel.

On the symbolic use of Jerusalem Shulam says, "Most Christians praising Jerusalem are really thinking about heaven. Why? First, because they ignore actual, literal Jerusalem in order to use the Jerusalem-concept in their own theologies. Second, because the real Jerusalem falls so far short of the heavenly version." I agree with him: in the real Jerusalem, one has to worry about hauling away the garbage, building access roads, attracting industry, and dealing with the troubled relationships between various ethnic and religious groups in the city, not to mention the political situation.

This leads me to discuss the relationship Messianic Jews have with politics in Israel. Some Israeli Messianic Jews lean toward the parties that favor keeping the Land of Israel under Jewish sovereignty and united Jerusalem as Israel's capital. Others favor the peace process on the biblical ground that peacemakers are blessed (Matt. 5:9). Nevertheless, many Messianic Jews are not particularly political, because they regard politics as worldly and therefore either altogether unsuitable for believers or of secondary importance as compared with spiritual life. They would rather pray than be political activists.

Certainly the gospel places a higher priority on spiritual values such as peace than on physical ones such as land. In a different context Scripture says, "The kingdom of God is not meat and drink, but righteousness, peace and joy" (Rom. 14:17). Nevertheless, Yeshua's approach to priorities is not to set aside lesser values just because greater ones are emphasized. This is shown by his words at Matt. 23:23: "You pay your tithes of mint, dill and cumin; but you have neglected the weightier matters of the *Torah*—justice, mercy, trust. These are the things you should have attended to—without neglecting the others!" Moreover, from a biblically prophetic viewpoint "peace versus land" is an inappropriate pair of opposites, since the two cannot be separated. According to the New Testament, the Jewish people ("all the tribes") must be back in the Land of Israel when Yeshua returns to establish world peace: "Then the sign of the Son of Man will appear in the sky, all the tribes of the Land will mourn, and they will see the Son of Man coming on the clouds of heaven with tremendous power and glory" (Matt. 24:30, *Complete Jewish Bible*[3]).

At the same time, let me make these two points: (1) No matter how control over Jerusalem is apportioned by peace processes, the State of Israel is a democracy with laws guaranteeing equal rights, so that Bible-believers must support equal rights for all loyal residents and leave no room for second-class citizenship. (2) I believe that although God will in the end give the Land to the Jewish people—no matter what interim solutions the diplomats, politicians and generals come up with—nevertheless, the question of whether and/or to what degree a struggle for possession of the Land is justified biblically is one not easily answered to the satisfaction of all. Theologians have developed scriptural foundations for three mutually inconsistent views: pacifism, just war and holy war; but this is not the place to discuss them. I mention this only as a reminder that relating to Jerusalem is bound up with broader issues.[4]

To sum up: Messianic Jews are comfortable with the following significances for Jerusalem:

1. Jerusalem is the eternal capital of the Jewish nation, whom God is returning to the Land of Israel and to faith in her Messiah, Yeshua.
2. Jerusalem symbolizes Judaism, Jewish history and the Jewish people; it also symbolizes Christianity, Christian history and the Church. Messianic Jews have roots in both histories and affirm both aspects of Jerusalem's symbolic significance.
3. Jerusalem is the city to which Yeshua the Messiah will return. From there he will rule Israel and all the nations.
4. God's *Torah*, understood as including New Testament truth as well as that of the *Tanakh*, has gone forth, is going forth and will go forth from Jerusalem.
5. The first Messianic Jews lived in and ministered from Jerusalem. Today's Messianic Jews, as the believing remnant of the

Jewish people, have established a community there and intend to be part of the process of ministering *Torah* from Jerusalem.

6. Regardless of their political views, Messianic Jews generally agree that living for God is a more important value than holding onto territory. Nevertheless, God's promises to the Jews concerning territory—the Land of Israel and the city of Jerusalem—are not canceled and are not to be neglected.

If you visit Jerusalem's Church of the Holy Sepulchre, built over the site of Yeshua's crucifixion and resurrection, at a certain point your tour guide will stop and inform you that that particular spot is "the navel of the universe." This suggestive *midrash* (allegory) tells us that Jerusalem is regarded as the key to world history. Certainly the Bible substantiates that assessment. A secular confirmation is found in the fact that, after the megalopolises of New York and Washington, there are more newspaper reporters in Jerusalem, with its barely half a million persons, than in any other city in the world. Why does this city attract such attention? What is the world waiting for?

Bible-believers know. Yeshua the Messiah will return to this city to establish the Kingdom of God on earth. The day may be near or far, but we eagerly expect it. Meanwhile it is up to us to establish and demonstrate as much of God's rulership as his Spirit gives us the love, wisdom and strength to do. And while this can be done anywhere, it is from Jerusalem that God's *Torah*, his teaching, will go forth. Messianic Jews living in Jerusalem intend to be at the center of this process, proclaiming Yeshua's Messiahship and God's kingdom.

People ask if Jerusalem is "the city of peace." It surely will be. Even now Yeshua is fulfilling his word given in John 14:27, "Peace I leave with you, my peace I give unto you: not as the world giveth, give I unto you. Let not your heart be troubled, neither let it be afraid." Moreover, one day the Messiah will return to fulfill the meaning of one of his titles, *Sar Shalom*, Prince of Peace (Isa. 9:5–7). This will satisfy everyone who trusts in him, no matter what his religious background—Jewish, Christian, Muslim, or other. Meanwhile it behooves and benefits all of us to follow God's instruction given in Ps. 122:6, "Pray for the peace of Jerusalem: they shall prosper that love thee."

1. For a fuller discussion see David H. Stern, "The People of God, the Promises of God, and the Land of Israel," in this work.

2. Gershon Nerel, *Messianic Jews in Eretz-Israel (1917-1967): Trends and Changes in Shaping Self-Identity*, Jerusalem, 1995.

3. David H. Stern, *Complete Jewish Bible* (Clarksville, Maryland: Jewish New Testament Publications, Inc., 1998). This is the combination of the *Tanakh* (Old Testament) and my translation of the New Testament in a way that brings out its inherent Jewishness. In the cited passage Yeshua is alluding to the "tribes of the Land" because the phrase is quoted from Zech. 12:11, where the context is the Land of Israel, not the whole earth.

4. For a wide-ranging discussion of many aspects of Jerusalem—its history, geography, archeology, use in the arts and religious significance—see the 215-page article on it in the *Encyclopedia Judaica* (Jerusalem: Keter Publishing House, 1971), volume 9, pp. 1378-1593.

ISRAEL AND PROPHECY

Louis Goldberg

Words in our language run in familiar pairs: lox and bagels, corn beef on rye bread, borscht and sour cream; husband and wife, brother and sister, and so on. Israel's sages, while defining one aspect of the soul as unique, contrast it to the limbs of the body which run in pairs (Midrash Genesis Rabbah 14:9).

In the same way, one pair of words go together naturally: *Israel and Prophecy.* What is Israel without prophecy? How can we speak of Israel and omit altogether the revelation of God, or even minimize the Word of God, especially those portions which have prophetic import for Israel. Israel and prophecy must go together. On the other hand, how can one speak of prophecy without also at the same time mentioning Israel. A small number of prophecies are present regarding individuals in the Hebrew Scriptures, which have no relation to Israel; the Torah, or Word, also has a number of prophecies as to the Messiah. But prophecy in its fullest scope must include the people of Israel as well as the land of Israel. Israel without prophecy has no meaning.

This pair of terms is also a reminder that present in the Bible is a discernible *philosophy of history.* What is history apart from what can be ascertained through the revelation of God? Figures of dates, and names of men? One can relate various events which have occurred because of cause and effect within the movement of history. As a result, such occurrences may suggest a number of theories to account for the ebb and flow of history, but when the theorizing has yielded some conclusions, history still has a way of appearing disjointed and without any specific goal. Humanistic views of history do not have what is called *telos,* or purpose, or possible end result. The Word, however, does present purpose in the movement of history with an end result which God has definitely in mind.

This revelation of God becomes necessary to reveal this purpose within history so as to make it meaningful.

The means by which we comprehend this philosophy of history is seen in the purposes of God for Israel, and central to these purposes are the covenants or specific agreements God has with Israel. Whether one will admit it or not, these covenants place Israel at the very core of history and focus on some of the purposes in the historical processes God has in mind. The balance of this discussion will concern itself with the agreements which are in full force from today's point of view, and which will have even greater meaning in the days ahead as history unfolds.

Abrahamic Agreement

The initial prophecy in the observation is the Abrahamic covenant where the patriarch was uniquely encountered on special occasions. This covenant is the first in a series that will ultimately unfold a number of purposes to provide direction within history. In each of the agreements, God made a statement to define the covenant, and then spelled out the terms.

The Statement to Abraham

With regard to Abraham, God took the initiative and said, "I will confirm my covenant between me and you" (Gen. 17:2).[1] With the proclamation of this statement, the terms follow to reveal some of the purposes God has in mind for peoples in the Middle East and particular, the people Israel.

A Progeny

God proceeded to delineate Abraham's descendants, stating, "I will multiply you exceedingly," and "I will make you exceedingly fruitful" (Gen. 17:2, 6). The first of these terms describes the patriarch's descendants, so numerous they will be without number. One needs to remember that this promise has no limit to just one family of descendants, but rather is a general term which applies to all the seed of Abraham.

The term specifies Isaac as well as the line that extends to Jacob and the descendants which came from Jacob. But this does not exclude the other son of Abraham, Ishmael. Of this other son, God said, "And as for Ishmael, I have heard you: I will surely bless him; greatly increase his numbers . . ." (Gen. 17:20).

One also notes the number of grandchildren and other components of the offspring: 1) Isaac had two sons, Jacob and Esau (Gen. 25:23), and Ishmael had twelve sons (Gen. 25:13). Esau's descendants became the Edomites (Gen. 36:10–29). And, after Sarah died, Abraham had six other sons of Keturah (Gen. 25:2). Even Lot's descendants can be included as well since he is related to Abraham, even though Lot's two daughters were despicable enough in the way they insured a line for themselves (Gen. 19:37, 38). Their two sons became Moab and Amon who have their part in the Middle East also. Therefore, as one examines this first term of exceeding fruitfulness, the total seed of Abraham needs to be considered.

As this term unfolded itself in the process within history, two main elements of progeny develop. One, the line of Isaac and Jacob and the latter's descendants, today comprising the Jewish people. The other line was made up of all the descendants of Ishmael's sons, Esau's sons, and Lot's grandchildren as well as the six sons with Keturah in later life. Many of these intermarried and became, for all practical purposes, the Arab peoples within the borders from the Mediterranean to Jordan, and perhaps also the territory of northwest Arabia as we know it today. Many of these Arab peoples have emigrated to areas all over the Middle East as well as in Western Europe and North America.

So, in a general sense, then, all the seed of Abraham must be included in the first general term to comprise Jewish and those Arab peoples living generally in the territories mentioned above.

Nations and Kings
The next of the terms of the Abrahamic covenant mentions nations and kings (Gen. 17:4–6). Again it is a general term that applies to all of the seed of Abraham. Of the line of Isaac and Jacob, and in the ensuing development of the nation, many illustrious kings arose, for example, David, Solomon, Asa, Jehoshaphat, Hezekiah and Josiah, and so on. Some of these kings were spiritually minded, guiding people into spiritual revival.

But illustrious kings were also present on the other side of the line. Concerning Ishmael, God stated, ". . . He will be the father of twelve rulers, and I will make him a great nation" (Gen. 17:20). Other sons fathered peoples who became nations as well as a number of rulers. What is frequently overlooked is that the Arab peoples have played their part in the history of mankind, as for example, their contribution of culture and learning through their philosophers, scientists, and writers to Western Europe when it was going through the depths of the Middle Ages. So what God said to Abraham in his agreement is that he would make his descendants into nations with well known rulers, and a glance at history verifies this promise.

An Everlasting Covenant with One People

In the third term of this covenant, God also announced to Abraham, "And I will establish My covenant as an everlasting covenant between me and you and your descendants after you for the generations come, to be your God and the God of your descendants after you" (Gen. 17:7). In a very general way, this is a promise which again applies to all of the descendants of Abraham, both Arab and Jewish people.

One must take note, now, that a particularization has entered into the picture. The unfolding of this term reveals a special word which sets apart the line of Isaac and Jacob, which is explained, "Yes, but Sarah your wife will bear you a son, and you will call him Isaac. I will establish my covenant with him as an everlasting covenant for his descendants after him" (Gen. 17:19). The statement is further emphasized, "But My covenant I will establish with Isaac, whom Sarah will bear to you by this time next year" (Gen. 17:21). The message is specially tailored to demonstrate a contrast between Isaac and Ishmael. Note also how this promise is further stated to Isaac (Gen. 26:4).

In the third generation, after Abraham and Isaac, the term is further narrowed within this agreement: God's Word says, not only to Abraham and uniquely to Isaac, but also finally in particularization with Jacob, "Your name will no longer be Jacob, but Israel . . ." (Gen. 32:28; see also Gen. 35:9), and then the Word adds concerning the patriarch Israel, "I am God Almighty; be fruitful and increase in number. A nation and a community of nations will come from you, and kings will come from your body" (Gen. 35:11). Since this is a continuation of the Abrahamic agreement, already promised to Isaac, God also promised his continued presence with the line of Isaac, as well as Jacob, for as long as the human race exists.

Israel will always be present because God's hand will always be upon them. Jewish people have suffered greatly at certain periods in history, but they have never been expunged from the human race. Some might not like the decisions of the State of Israel, but the presence of Abraham's Almighty God is with Israel because of a promise he made with Abraham, Isaac and Jacob.

In general, most of the descendants on the other side of the line, the Arab peoples, are still present to this day as well. Palestinian Arabs will refer to the Israeli Jews as "our first cousins," and some Israeli Jews refer to the Arabs as "our half brothers." The recognition exists that both peoples come from a common ancestor.

The only exception among Abraham's other side were the descendants of Esau, the Edomites. God put a curse on them for the way they treated the people Israel when they came out of Egypt on their way to their promised land when Edom's leaders and soldiers would not let them pass through their land (Num. 20:14–21). Later, God expressed his disgust with Edom for their pride in their possessions, the lands and homes carved out of the living rock high in the hills. He mentioned again how they treated their brethren when they were on the way in the wilderness and so he put a curse on them (Obad. vss. 3–14). Finally, when Judah had fallen to Babylon and the Temple in Jerusalem lay in ruins, Edom took great glee with the misfortune of their brethren and occupied some of the land of Judah. God's wrath was directed against them and again he promised they eventually would no longer be remembered (Ezek. 36:1–7). In the course of time, the Edomites disappeared altogether and no one lives in the areas they once occupied.

The Promise of Land
The last term of this covenant referred to a piece of land in the Middle East: "On that day the Lord made a covenant with Abram and said, 'To your descendants I give this land, from the river of Egypt to the great river, the Euphrates'" (Gen. 15:18). All of Abraham's people are to live in a certain geographical area, but the line of Isaac and Jacob have their land specified.

The question can be asked as to whether this land is for all the seed of Abraham or not. A further directive is provided to Isaac (Gen. 26:2, 3), specifying a particular piece of land. Then this promise if further extended to Jacob concerning this same special land, "The land I gave to Abraham and Isaac I also give to you, and I give the land to your descendants after you" (Gen. 35:12).

A piece of real estate is associated with this covenant in perpetuity that applies to the line of Isaac and Jacob. The question of Jacob's or Israel's right to this land is settled on the basis of God's Word and this argument should be sufficient insofar as believers are concerned.

People also have asked, "What about the other side of the line? Do not Abraham's descendants on the other line have a land?" Assuredly a phrase is present which appears to answer this question in a very general way. When Abraham settled the inheritance claims for his six sons, he gave gifts to the sons of Keturah (Gen. 25:6). Then he sent them away from his son Isaac to the land of the east. Since God spelled out the specific land that was to belong to the line of Isaac and Jacob, then the very general distinction, "Land of the east," is taken to mean the rest of the Middle East. But please note carefully that the Middle East is the home for all the seed of Abraham, the seed of Jacob having its particular share.

David's Agreement

The second major agreement God made with Israel, which is still ongoing, was the promise to David concerning a coming kingdom. While implications of this covenant could have been fulfilled when Yeshua the Messiah had come, the full meaning of the terms of this agreement will yet take place on this earth.

The Statement of the Covenant

After David had come to a point in his ministry, he mused as to what should be done for the ark which was housed in a tent like structure. He thought of providing a more permanent well-designed building to house the tabernacle, but Nathan the prophet received other plans regarding any future special building.

After God revealed his will to Nathan, he came to David and instructed him regarding the Davidic covenant. As with the

Abrahamic promise, God took the initiative to instruct him regarding this new agreement (2 Sam. 7:12–16). David's son, Solomon, was to eventually be the rightful heir to the throne and build the Temple. It would be of his line that the Messiah would come.

The three terms of this agreement—house, kingdom and throne—have a far-reaching implication (vs. 16) that even David did not understand. He exclaimed, "Who am I, O Sovereign Lord, what is my family, that you have brought me this far?" (2 Sam. 7:18) God revealed that of the line of David will be a special house with descendants; a kingdom will yet come over which David's descendants will reign; and a throne will also exist upon which David's descendants, especially the Messiah, will yet sit.

The House of David Through Solomon
As David's line is traced, an interesting facet of God's promise is revealed. The historical kingdom of the Old Testament ended with the disruption of the First Commonwealth when the Solomonic Temple was destroyed by the Babylonians in 586 B.C.E. While no kings of the house of David ruled in the Second Commonwealth, commencing with the inception of the second Temple in 536 B.C.E., the line of David never ceased.[2] At the end of the second Temple period, in the first century C.E., Yeshua the Messiah appeared. Both Matthew and Luke carefully traced his genealogy back to David.

But Joseph, his "father," could not be linked biologically to Yeshua because of the curse on the line of Solomon. He had the right to pass on the inheritance rights of the line of kings, and yet, any direct link with Yeshua could not be possible. Miriam's (Mary) genealogy provides the necessary link to David because as the line is traced, it goes back to a brother of Solomon, Nathan (1 Chron. 3:5), and then, to David. Therefore, Miriam provides the identity with David and the kingly line, avoiding the curse, while Joseph passed on the rights to kingship.

Throne of Solomon from David
Again, the throne of Solomon was occupied throughout the First Commonwealth, until the last leader, Zedekiah, actually only a prince once the curse had been placed on the line. In the second commonwealth, no king ruled of the Solomonic house, and

therefore the throne remained unoccupied. Yeshua the Messiah had the right to sit upon that throne and could have commenced his reign, after his death as an atonement for sin,[3] *if the Sanhedrin had acknowledged him as King-Messiah.* He had all the credentials for doing so, proving his identity by both word and deed. Tragically, no positive decision was rendered by the Sanhedrin, and thereafter, throughout the age of the body of the Messiah, the throne of David remains unoccupied, as it will until the day when all Israel will accept their true Messiah and King.

The Kingdom of Peace Yet to Come

Since Yeshua was of the house of David, he had authority to rule in the kingdom that God promised to David, as well as to the nation Israel. David's greater son has this honored position which God promised, not only based on the prophecy in 2 Samuel Chapter 7, but in other prophecies as well. While the fullness of this kingdom has not yet taken place, the day is yet to come when the fulfillment will occur, at which time Yeshua will take his rightful place on the throne of David.

Again, one sees the divine purpose to which God is moving history, and some day a Messianic kingdom will exist over which David's son will sit on his throne and reign; it will be a kingdom consisting not only of Israel alone, but will also include the nations of the earth. A political ideology of kingdom and king might not be compatible with the current government, that is, rulership by the people. But in the kingdom yet to come, God's purpose is that David's greater son will rule over his kingdom on this earth to insure justice and righteousness and peace among nations.

So, in God's design, the word to David and the terms of this covenant spell out the perpetuity of his throne, his house and his kingdom that will one day see their greatest fulfillment amid conditions for which men have always longed.

The New Covenant

In still another agreement that has consequences for Israel and all peoples, a special word was given to the prophet Jeremiah that spelled out important considerations for the kingdom that would affect spiritual, moral and physical conditions in preparation for the kingdom of peace.

The Statement of the New Covenant

The New Covenant to be made with Israel and Judah has some far reaching implications:

> "The time is coming," declares the Lord,
> "when I will make a new covenant
> with the house of Israel
> and with the house of Judah . . ."

> "This is the covenant I will make with the house of
> Israel after that time," declares the Lord.
> (Jer. 31:31, 33)

Again God took the initiative to announce his intentions for his people Israel, in a similar action as with the Abrahamic and Davidic covenants. It now remains to consider the terms of this covenant.

The Mosaic Constitution

God had given Israel the Mosaic constitution as well as a kingship. He gave his people every opportunity to develop spiritually and morally under this Mosaic contract. No question should ever be raised about the integrity of this constitution. Many people attempt to live within its principles of righteousness and justice; every opportunity was present within this agreement to know the Lord and to living godly for him. The testimony to God's faithfulness can be seen in the lives of the remnant in every generation.

Tragically, some very real problems also existed. At times many of the people lived on a low spiritual level, or the kings were not godly. The prophets were well aware of the poor quality of lifestyle. Not only did they preach to their respective generations concerning their failures in living the principles of justice, equity and righteousness within the Mosaic constitution, but they also began to spell out the days of the coming prophetic Messianic kingdom. Within the parameters of this new kingdom, people were pictured as knowing the Lord. The king would be a perfect one, David's greater son, the Messiah. He would be the most excellent king, ruling in a utopia, not initiated by men but instituted by God himself. Therefore, the prophet stressed that the New Covenant will not be "like the covenant made with the fathers" (Jer. 31:32); an entire new set of conditions will be set in place.

Possibility of Fulfillment

All during Yeshua's ministry, he demonstrated his claims to Messiah by his work and teaching. Finally he presented his messianic credentials to the High Priest. When the High Priest asked him, "I charge you under oath by the living God: Tell us if you are the Messiah, the Son of God" (Matt. 26:63), Yeshua paraphrased what Daniel had written and applied it to his own identity (Matt. 26:64; Dan. 7:13). His answer left no doubt in the High Priest's mind as to what he was saying, but his words are so unique that the only interpretation could be his ability to bring in this kingdom. If Israel could have accepted Jesus as the Messiah, atonement would have been made for sin, and the kingdom could have been instituted.[4]

Perhaps at least 20% of the nation, by the end of the first century, did accept Yeshua as the Messiah.[5] We must never forget that the "flower of the early body of Messiah" was Jewish believers who affirmed their hope in Yeshua as the Messiah of Israel.

The tragedy is that the leadership of the nation brought about a negative divine decision. Some forty years later in 70 C.E., when the Herodian Temple was destroyed, bringing the second Temple period to an end, and after the second revolt against Rome in 135 C.E., a world wide dispersion of Israel began. After the Arab invasion in the early 600s and Arabization of the land, more and more Jewish people left. However, even though they scattered, God never forsook Israel. The possibility always existed for peace of mind and heart by receiving Yeshua. Many times the unregenerate within Christendom and even ungodly Gentile believers did untold and indescribable harm to Jewish people. Yet God always had individual believers who loved Jewish people and in humility shared the Messiah Yeshua. We will rejoice one day because of the great numbers of Jewish people who found Messiah during the period of the *galut* (dispersion.)

Present Preparation of Israel

The present day is an amazing period. God will not be thwarted in his purposes. He will yet establish the fullness of this New Covenant and a word from the prince of the prophets serves as a reminder of what God will do for Israel to keep his word:

> In that day the Lord will reach out his hand a second time to reclaim the remnant that is left of his people from Assyria, from Lower Egypt, from Upper Egypt, from Cush, from Elam, from Babylonia, from Hamath and from the islands of the sea.
>
> He will raise a banner for the nations and will gather the exiles of Israel; he will assemble the scattered people of Judah from the four quarters of the earth. (Isa. 11:11, 12)

A First Dispersion and Regathering
The fascinating phrase, "the second time," is interesting to pursue. When Isaiah wrote this, it was about 700 B.C.E., one hundred and twenty years before Jerusalem was sacked and Judah lost her Temple. Therefore, one can assert that Judah experienced its first great dispersion when the First Commonwealth came to an end in 536 B.C.E. But, as predicted by Jeremiah the prophet (25:10, 11; 29:10), a remnant of the Jewish people returned to Judah in 538 B.C.E. after Cyrus the Persian and his armies attacked and subjugated Babylon the previous year. The 500s B.C.E. reveal a first dispersion and first regathering of Jewish people.

The Second Dispersion
Jewish people lived in the land under the Second Commonwealth until 70 C.E. when the Romans besieged the city of Jerusalem and destroyed the Second Temple. They then began a dispersion over some six hundred years, this time not just to one specific area but to a world wide dispersion. The *galut* continued until the latter 1800s, and now in the days in which we live, that can be described as "the second time" of regathering.

Details Concerning the Second Regathering
Modern Israel began about 1860 when a few hardy Jewish people moved out of the Old City of Jerusalem and started a new settlement destined to become the new part of Jerusalem. Also, because of the increasing intensity of the pogroms in Eastern Europe, beginning in 1881–82, a trickle of emigration occurred to the land of

Israel (although the bulk of Jewish emigration out of this area, from 1880–1914, about 2,000,000, went to the United States). This small emigration to Israel, however, took place at least sixteen years before a formal Zionist Congress took place. The old leaders in Israel, Ben Gurion, Levi Eshkol, etc., were the pioneers who followed this emigration from Eastern Europe, but in time, the trickle of emigration was destined to increase.

Moreover, there were many articles on returning to Israel, by writers of various persuasions, secular and religious, from the 1840s to the end of that century. In what can be described as a work of the Holy Spirit, each one was led to tell Jewish people that the time had come to return to the homeland. The essays became instrumental in the call by Herzl for the first Zionist Congress in 1897 in Basle, Switzerland.

At the well known trial of Captain Dreyfuss, of the French army, who was accused by the military hierarchy of selling France's state secrets to Germany, sat a young reporter from Vienna, Theodore Herzl. As he understood the proceedings of the first trial, which eventuated in a court martial of Dreyfuss and sentence to Devil's Island, he began to realize that if this terrible outbreak of anti-Jewishness can happen in the land of liberty, equality and fraternity, if this is what was to be the reward for Jewish contribution in Western Europe, then there could be no more future for the Jew in Western Europe![6] Herzl's book, *The Jewish State*, and the emergence of anti-Jewish feeling, led to the first Zionist congress in 1897 which thereafter spurred the emigration of Jewish people to the land of Israel.

England's Interest "For and Against"
World War I came, and in 1917 the British made an offer in the Balfour declaration to make Palestine a homeland for the Jews. The move was providential because once it was ratified in 1922, along with other decisions concerning the end of the war, it would be only ten years before the rise of Nazi power in Germany. One senses a divine means to provide a place where German Jews, and other European Jews, could flee during the 1930s when Hitler was to apply his pressure and repression against Jewish people.

In 1936 the Arabs in British Palestine rioted against this immigration of Jewish people in increasing numbers from Germany and

Austria, and Britain attempted to honor both peoples in an attempt at a solution. Not being able to come to terms with both, the British made their decision outlined in the White Paper Act of 1939: emigration of Jewish people was to be limited to only 10,000 a year to a maximum of 50,000 in five years, with an additional 25,000 to demonstrate British "grace," after which no more emigrants would be permitted. True, at the outbreak of World War II, England did not want problems with the Palestinian Arabs, but in a time when Jewish people needed a place to go, they were barred from the land of Israel except for the pittance of 10,000 per year, this in the face of a rising elimination of Jews. During World War II, the hostility simmered between Arab and Jew but it broke out again when World War II was over, making the situation in the land of Israel even more desperate. The White Paper was in force when thousands of refugees, somehow surviving the death camps, were trying to enter Israel. England finally could not handle the desperate political situation between Jewish and Arab peoples any more, and the conflict was placed into the hands of the United Nations. After studying the situation, the world body recommended a division of the land where Jewish people would have their portion and the Palestinian Arabs would have their part as well. Israel accepted the plan, the Arabs rejected it, and the rest is now history. On May 15, 1948 the State of Israel came into existence and the tragic Arab-Israel war was on.

In the mysterious council of God, this Arab-Israel confrontation was a divine call for Sephardi Jews in Arab countries in North Africa and Oriental Jews in Arab countries in the Middle East, to return home to Israel. In the period between 1948–1960 almost a million and a half Jews emigrated to the homeland. Within the permissive will of God, a sizable number of Jews were nudged back to the land of their forefathers. In addition, Jewish people also came, from the camps in Europe, as well as from many countries in Europe. Today, at least one half of the population in Israel is comprised of Jewish people from Arab countries.

The Six Day War in 1967, aside from the military conflict, needs to be seen as a catalyst. This war stirred the hearts of young Jewish people in the United States and Canada who realized their attachment to the homeland of Israel and the preservation of the state. Between 1967–1973 about 50,000 from North America emigrated, and while some did return, most remained in Israel.

This war also had an effect on Soviet Jewry, and they took decisive action to leave for the homeland. Since the Israeli victory was galling to the Soviet authorities, the latter found a target to attack: not Jewish people per se, but Zionism. With the attack on this concept, Soviet Jews felt they were being singled out for special persecution.

The Soviets at this time desperately wanted favorite trading status with the United States, but the price demanded by the latter was that if peoples desired to freely emigrate, they should have the right to do so. Obviously, such a concept was anathema to the Soviet authorities, but so willing were they for this status, they relented on their policy of no emigration. As a result, and because of the immediate catalyst of the war, some 100,000 Soviet Jews were able to get out of the Soviet Union between 1967 to 1973 and emigrate to Israel. In 1973, the bars rang down again and hardly anyone was able to emigrate anywhere.

But God was again "to stir the pot" in the Soviet Union when the monolithic system of communism collapsed in 1990. With all restrictions out of the way, at least a million Jewish people left, some to the United States and elsewhere, but at least 500,000 went to Israel between 1990 and 1993. And, at this writing, they are still coming to Israel at the rate of some 30,000 a year.

Therefore, as we speak of a regathering, the Scriptural phrase, "the second time," has great significance. These are the days of "the second time" when, beginning with 1880, only 25,000 Jewish people were present in the land of Israel, and, in the intervening years until this writing, one sees the gathering of Jewish people from the four corners of the earth to the homeland. The current population is slightly more than five million, and if the trend continues from the former Soviet Union, Israel's population will exceed that of the United States. We would have to be blind not to realize a movement of God in the last almost 120 years. What is amazing is to walk the streets of Jerusalem, Tel Aviv, Haifa, Tiberius, Ashdod, Ashkelon, Beer Sheva and many of the other cities in Israel and look at the faces of the youngsters being reared in the homeland. One realizes that God's hand has moved historical events of nations to effect this return. But we can ask ourselves the question: What will God yet do in the United States to move Jewish people back to the homeland?

Establishing the New Covenant
When the New Covenant in its totality of spiritual (Jer. 31:33, 34) as well as material blessings (Jer. 31:10–12, 23, 24, 28) was not established when Messiah came the first time, the purposes of the Lord were not fully thwarted. God brought the body of the Messiah into existence, open to Jewish people and Gentiles, to enjoy the totality of spiritual blessings (Eph. 1:3).

As this age comes to a close, the Lord will take the body of Messiah out of this world, and turn again to work through the people of Israel.[7] The New Covenant will be established and consummated with its spiritual and physical blessings with Israel after a tremendous holocaust in the Land (the time of Jacob's trouble, Zech. 13:8, 9). In the days of the fullness of the New Covenant, a generation of Israelis will enter into a new spiritual experience with the Lord, as described,

> ". . . But this is the covenant I will make with the house of Israel after that time," declares the Lord. "I will put my law in their minds and write it on their hearts.
> I will be their God, and they will be My people.
> No longer will a man teach his neighbor, or a man his brother, saying, 'Know the Lord,' because they will all know Me, from the least of them to the greatest," declares the Lord. "For I will forgive their wickedness and will remember their sins no more."
> (Jer. 31:33, 34)

The prophet continues to discuss physical aspects of this covenant which can only apply to a literal Israel: The existence of Israel is linked to the stability of the very laws that govern the movement of the universe. If one were to destroy the universe, or juggle its governing laws, then the agreement with the nation would be destroyed, thereby ending her existence (Jer. 31:35–37). Jerusalem is also included in this discussion which guarantees the continued existence of Israel's capital city which will one day be the diplomatic center of the world (Jer. 31:38–40).

When a New Covenant is ratified with Israel in the not too distant future, promised by God in the Hebrew Scriptures, the kingdom will be effected when David's greater son will come again as the nation of Israel receives Yeshua as the Messiah.

Spiritual Preparation

God's purposes also include spiritual preparation among people in the land of Israel, which is even more amazing than the providential movement of God among the nations. The Hebrew Scriptures is a subject in the primary and secondary schools in Israel and, from first to twelfth grades, young people spend four to six hours of study in the Hebrew Scriptures. In addition, many students take courses on the New Testament in the universities. Why this latter interest? The answer is not slow in coming: How can one live in Israel and avoid Yeshua? One "bumps" into him in many places where he taught and performed miracles. Israelis see the importance of knowing something about him who is one of Israel's great teachers, and yes, even a prophet. Obviously, we would also affirm he is the Messiah, but one should not be surprised at the interest in Yeshua on the part of many Israelis. In this manner, through the human desire to effect ties with the people of 2000 years ago, God is working to prepare hearts for what is ahead.

When we talk about Israel and prophecy, these three covenants—Abrahamic, Davidic and New Covenant—need consideration. God has a purpose within history whereby he is moving Israel for a great rendezvous with the true Messiah.

I sat one night in one of the main halls in Jerusalem and heard the Chief of Chaplains, Shlomo Goren. For 45 minutes, he spoke of biblical materials that relate to these days. With his soft eyes, a face framed by a gray beard, standing as though an Old Testament prophet had stepped out of the pages of the Scriptures, he said to the audience, "These are the days of the footsteps of the Messiah. There are dark days ahead but there is no turning back. The day is coming," he affirmed with conviction, "when the Messiah will come here and the kingdom will begin." Can you imagine the effect on the audience as they listened to this rabbi? One cannot afford to close his eyes to what God is doing with the people of Israel today.

The terms Israel and Prophecy belong together.

1. Scripture citations are from the New International Version unless otherwise noted.

2. A very valid reason exists why no kings ruled in the second commonwealth. God had placed a curse on the line of Solomon, beginning with Jehoiachin (Jer. 22:24–30). For that reason, none of the rightful heirs of Solomon ruled as king, but instead, the priests took the leadership of the nation.

3. If the Sanhedrin had accepted Yeshua as king over Israel, the Romans would have considered such a decision as a breach of trust; they would have deposed the leaders and even ordered them put to death, and for sure, they would have crucified Yeshua, thinking they could and any pretension to leadership by him. Upon his resurrection, however, God would have cared for the Romans in his most inimitable action.

4. As already noted, the Romans would have killed Yeshua anyway and thereby, the atonement would have taken place, and his resurrection would have been the proof of his integrity

5. One notes some of the figures, 3,000 (Acts 2:41), 5,000 men (Acts 4:4), great number of priests became believers (Acts 7), literally, myriads (tens) of thousands by the end of Paul's journey (Acts 21:20), and between 70–100, because of the loss of the Temple, such a window of opportunity existed for the Jewish believers in Yeshua to explain that he had predicted that such a catastrophe would indeed occur in Israel, and a good possibility exists that many became believers because of this testimony.

6. Only the efforts to exonerate Dreyfuss by Emile Zola in his book *J'Accuse* (which had to be published in England, so fierce was the anti-Jewish sentiment) was world opinion brought to bear on France's leaders. Dreyfuss was brought back for a second trial and only the intervention of France's president spared this French Jewish captain from the possibility of a conviction at this new trial. Dreyfuss did return to the army, fully reinstated, but to this day, the details of what brought about the trial are still considered top secret.

7. Not everyone will agree with this eschatology, but this writer will assert that not all of what Jeremiah had promised has reached its fulfillment. In this age, we enjoy all spiritual blessings (Heb. 8:5–12), but the prophet had predicted a totality of spiritual and physical blessings for the kingdom, which will yet occur when Israel is ready to receive their rightful king. See Louis Goldberg, *Turbulence Over the Middle East* (Neptune, NJ: Loizeaux, 1982).

PRACTICAL MATTERS FOR MESSIANIC JEWS AND NON-JEWS

THE PROBLEM OF ASSIMILATION IN AMERICA

Patrice Fischer

Introduction

The struggle to survive has been the chief goal of much of Jewish history. This struggle might sometimes have been against "spiritual powers," but most times it has been against "flesh and blood." In recent times, unfortunately, the Jews' worst enemy has been their own apathy about their spiritual heritage. The problem is not just in the quality of Jewish life but the actual decrease in *numbers* of Jews across the world.

From a sociological viewpoint this dwindling population is regrettable. The scholars within the Jewish community have written numerous articles on the problem of assimilation—the process by which Jews lose their distinctive "Jewishness" through intermarriage with Gentiles and their neglect of their religious observance. Statistics show that out of 14 million Jews worldwide, less than one-fourth attend synagogue once a week, and forty percent are relatively disengaged from Jewish life.[1]

A study of worldwide Jewish assimilation far exceeds the space limitations of this volume. This paper, therefore, will center on the American Jewish community, which at six million strong is about twenty percent larger than the population of Israel. The forces to assimilate within American culture are the strongest the Jewish people have ever had to face. The "melting pot" mentality of the United States invites acceptance into the mainstream of society at the price of giving up ethnic loyalties and ties.

> Every ethnic minority is subjected to two conflicting tendencies, the isolating and the assimilating . . . The assimilating tendencies consist of those

economic and cultural factors that create for the minority the necessity and the will to dissolve within the majority.[2]

It is this process that will be examined. After some preliminary theological considerations, a short history of Jews in America is presented to provide an historical context. The statistics behind assimilation are presented, and then some steps toward solutions within a Messianic context are explored.

Theology of Jewish Survival

Jeremiah was known as "the weeping prophet" because of his burden of announcing to Judah its impending destruction. Through him God voices his anger at the Jewish people on the eve of the destruction of Jerusalem by the Babylonians. Among the sins of the day were widespread idolatry, governmental corruption, false religiosity instead of true faith, false prophecies by self-seeking prophets, oppression of the poor and orphaned, and self-pride. The description of the nation's condition and God's displeasure is among the most frightening in the *Tanakh* (Old Testament).

Yet in the midst of this horror, God chooses to preserve the Jewish people. This would have been an ideal time to destroy them all and start again, and yet God's promise to preserve the Jews remains true. In the first six chapters verse after verse condemns the Jewish people of the day in scathing terms. Interspersed throughout this section is the mercy of God: "For thus says the LORD, 'The whole land shall be a desolation; yet I will not make a full end'" (Jer. 4:27). "'But even in those days,' says the LORD, 'I will not make a full end of you'" (Jer. 5:18).

In one of the most inspiring sections of the Scriptures—Jer. 31–33—God pledges the survival of the Jewish people forever:

> Thus says the LORD, who gives the sun for light by day and fixed order of the moon and the stars for light by night . . . If this fixed order departs from before me, says the Lord, then shall the descendants of Israel cease from being a nation before me forever. (Jer. 31:35–36)

God has firmly committed himself to the continuing existence of the Jewish people, regardless of any shortcomings on their part.

A Judaism without Jews is not what God wishes, just as theology without flesh to carry it out is unthinkable. But all too often we expect God to perform miracles to make things right without any willingness on our part to do his will here on earth as he has shown us. This is particularly true in the case of Jewish survival. All those who take the biblical record seriously should make the preservation of the Jewish people a priority.

Given the importance of Jewish survival in the world today, what has been the history of American assimilation for Jews?

America: Land of Promise

There has been a Jewish community in America since 1654, when 23 Jews from Brazil fled the Inquisition there by the new Portuguese colonizers. While other individual Jews had come before this time, this group was the first "community" to settle here.

The economy that America developed did not prohibit Jewish participation, so with the development of free capitalism, the Jews came. Their settlement in America can be roughly divided into four periods:

1654–1840	the S'fardic (Spanish/Mediterranean);
1841–1880	the German;
1881–1920	the Eastern European;
1920–present	the National (greatly restricted through quotas).[3]

In each case poor living conditions along with increased restrictions on the Jewish people provided the impetus for their immigration.

The S'fardic families who settled here brought their S'fardic synagogues. They settled among many colonial cities on the Eastern seaboard. With the coming of large numbers of German Jews in the 1840s came a new "branch" of Judaism, the Reform movement. This was a movement in Germany which had been developed first of all to adapt the Jewish beliefs to the "newest scientific thought," and also to hold back those converting out of Judaism by modernizing its practices.[4]

The Jewish integration into American society had started, and it attracted many. In 1840 there were 15,000 Jews in the U.S. By 1880 there were 250,000. This number increased dramatically because of immigrations from Eastern Europe, reaching 2,000,000 by World War I. They came as a result of increased anti-Semitism, particularly in Russia. There the policy of the Czarist government was death for one-third of the Jewish population, conversion for the second one-third and exile for the final third.[5]

The Reform movement, which was growing in popularity with the German Jewish population here, was not accepted by the Eastern European immigrants. Many of them were strictly Orthodox and kept their religious laws with great fervor. But some saw what the Reform movement was doing. They did not want to be quite so "modern," and felt that they needed their own scholars to defend the Hebrew Bible from the higher criticism of the German scholars. On the other hand, the Orthodoxy of the recent immigrants seemed stifling and was enmeshed in services spoken in Hebrew. As a result, "Conservative" synagogues were formed in 1913, with 16 organizing themselves into the United Synagogues of America. Their goal was to rejuvenate the Orthodox Eastern European congregations and also to oppose the much older and more powerful group of Reform synagogues.[6]

By the time of the mass immigration from Eastern Europe, most of the German Jews had become acculturated into American life. The three branches of Judaism—Reform, Conservative, and Orthodox—took their places in serving their particular sectors of the Jewish community. The Reform and Conservative branches in particular welcomed the merging of Jewish and American lifestyles as an aid to making the immigrants "feel at home" in their new land.

The period of 1920 to 1940 was one of great social turmoil in the Jewish community. As America's industry increased in technical development, immigrants serving as cheap labor were no longer needed. The Johnson Act in 1921 and the National Origins Act in 1924 sharply curtailed immigration. With these restrictions the flow of rabbis and Jewish leadership from Europe was cut off. This required the American community to provide their own seminaries (called *yeshivas*) and organizations to combine efforts for fund-raising and social action.

At the same time the economic status of the American Jewish community was steadily rising.

> They were transformed from a community of workers into a largely middle-class, white-collar population, including many businessmen and professionals. This was made possible by the increasing opportunity in the service fields in America.[7]

This enabled the American Jews to help the needy Jews of Europe during the widespread economic depression of the time.

With the advent of Hitler and the Nazi regime sweeping through Europe, there were many needy Jews to help. But because of the quota restrictions placed in the '20s, many Jewish refugees from Nazism were refused entry into the U.S. This policy of the Roosevelt administration to avoid interference into German's "domestic problems" is documented carefully in Arthur Morse's book, *While Six Million Died.*[8]

While it is not clear whether the average Jew in America perceived the situation in Europe, it is clear that the discoveries of the Allied troops in liberating the concentration camps in 1945 came as unprecedented shock to American Jewry. This provided the impetus to a massive Zionist push among all branches of American Judaism. Theodore Herzl, the founder of the modern Zionist movement, had been correct: in 1896 he wrote that *nowhere* could the Jewish people be safe except in their own homeland.[9] The battle to open the doors of Palestine reached an acute stage. After several years of illegal immigration by Jews, and terrorism within Palestine by both Arabs and Jews, the United Nations in 1948 partitioned the country into both an Arab and a Jewish state (Jordan and Israel). A war between the Arab states and Israel ensued to establish Israel's right to be a country, and eventually agreements were signed between the two opponents.

Thus the American Jewish community linked together the horrors of Europe in 1939–1945 with the establishment of Israel as a type of allegory: Israel dies that she might rise again. The survivors of Auschwitz (a term in this case used in synecdoche for the Holocaust as a whole) wanted the state of Israel because they refused to live again in "Christian Europe."[10]

American Jews had escaped the horrors of Hitler's "Final Solution," but this left them with a strange sense of guilt: "Why should we have been so fortunate, when our relatives suffered so much?" Their conscience was partially soothed, however, by the establishment of a homeland for the Jewish people. After all, American democracy was the friend of the Jews, or so they felt.

The State of Israel was caused by Christian Europe of nationalism and of racism, by the Europe which in most of its domains fell markedly short of achieving democracy. Had all the Jews of Europe come to the U.S. a century ago, as my parents did a half-century ago, and had America welcomed them as it received my parents, there would be no State of Israel today. It would not have been needed.[11]

America: Land of Assimilation

Jewish hearts in America were united in the realization of the Holocaust and the establishment of the state of Israel, and as a result became remarkably homogeneous in their social composition. As the occupations within the Jewish community continued to rise up the socio-economic ladder, the great impetus was to "become American," and yet to join a synagogue while doing so.[12]

There seemed to be a much greater interest in religion (as opposed to the quasi-national culture of Judaism) during the middle 1950s. One common explanation for this interest was the effect of both Hitler and Zionism. But Nathan Glazer claims that these two phenomena were not understood by the American Jewish community until the late 1950s.[13] Rather, the upsurge in religious interest lay in the more general category of "the move to the suburbs," which took place directly after the war years. American Jews joined much of middle class America in forming new communities on the outskirts of cities. Then as Jewish parents saw the need for Jewish education for their children, and community centers to meet in, these needs were remedied by building them with the increased money earned from higher paying jobs.[14] In the cities, as part of Jewish neighborhoods, it had been "easy" to be Jewish—everyone around was. Now Jews had to act like Jews: i.e., they had to do "Jewish things" so that they would be recognized as Jews by the Gentiles in their neighborhoods, and especially so that their Jewish children could learn how to be Jewish.

In one sense, the "melting pot" of American society turned out to be too much of a good thing for the Jewish community here. By the time of the 1960s, these "outcasts" of a previous era had achieved money, status, success, and power. They saw the emergence of Jews in every area of cultural activity: men such as Leonard Bernstein, Saul Bellow, Norman Mailer, Leon Uris. This was a reflection of a remarkable gain in personal freedom that the Jews as Jews had never known before. Eugene Borowitz calls the American Jews of the 1960s "the first free generation of Diaspora Jews."[15]

Sociologically, this was not surprising. As the American Jew fulfilled the "American dream," his values changed to become distinctively American and moved away from being distinctively Jewish.

> Since the Jews achieved the greatest economic and social success of all the immigrant groups, not surprisingly the process ended with the overwhelming bulk of American Jewry the most committed to integration and assimilation of American values.[16]

For the first time since the first century, Jews felt safe to be somewhere. Hence their distinctiveness was being lost.

> We Jews, sensitive to America's demands, terribly anxious to please, in order that we might find the safety we so desperately sought, came to view our relationship to America as contractual. In its extreme interpretation, the contract offered a promise of physical safety in return for a promise of cultural suicide. . . . Judaism as a faith, yes; Judaism as peoplehood, even if peoplehood was central to the faith, no.[17]

It was popular, and easy, to fit into American society, which "liked" Jews. But it was harmful to be "too Jewish." Secular attainments were to be admired.

> What the modern world did was to dissolve all the subordinate, supporting elements in Jewish identity. It broke down the geographical isolation of the

Jews. It created a culture with attractions and intellectual caliber which could not be dismissed as inferior. It exposed him to Gentiles, ethically and morally impressive (if not superior).[18]

The Sixties also brought the rise of social reform movements such as the NAACP and the civil rights movement. Anti-Semitism was at a low ebb, and Jews held leadership positions in many of the civil rights organizations. This trend was the result of the more liberal political and social outlook which is common among Jewish households. Meir Kahane says:

Jewish organizations and Jewish liberals in the past took upon their shoulders the task of freeing the black. Jews were at the forefront of the civil rights movement and Jewish groups were found at any time prepared to give money, bodies, and support for the black cause. They did so because it was one of the mythical Principles of the American Jew that Equality and Liberalism would save *him*. They were wrong. . . . The liberalism of Jewish organizations was born in the hope that it would save the Jew from anti-Semitism.[19]

As integration into American life continued, there arose a great drive in all the major faiths toward social action. The emphasis in American thought turned toward the modern, enlightened person for whom ethnic backgrounds make no difference—everyone wanted to be equal. Each person was striving to be a member of the "universal community of mankind." With the growth of the ecumenical movement in the Protestant churches and the convening of Vatican II in 1965, it was decided that the particulars which had divided people in the past were really unimportant. Emphasis would be placed on social action to bring this worldwide "oneness." Social action had been a Jewish strong point all along. Into this idyllic background burst the 1967 war in Israel.

The impact of the '67 war on American Jewry is too complex a topic to be treated adequately in an essay of this length.[20] But a few cursory remarks can be made concerning its effects.

> What the victory did do for us, and perhaps for
> most American Jews, was to reinforce a thousand-
> fold a new determination . . . It was a determina-
> tion to resist any who would in any way and to any
> degree and for any reason whatsoever attempt to
> do us harm, any who would diminish us or destroy
> us, any who would challenge our right and our
> duty to look after ourselves and our families, any
> who would deny us the right to pursue our own
> interests or frustrate us in our duty to do so.[21]

This rise in the identity consciousness of the American Jewish
community cannot be pictured too strongly. The silence of the
United States government during the war only underlined the silence of the world at large concerning Israel's right to exist. Even
more ominous were the echoes of the Holocaust being heard from
Arab leaders as they threatened to "push Israel into the sea." Once
again Jewish survival became the watchword of the day. The silence
of organized Christianity also stifled the dialogue that had just begun with Judaism.

However, the most important result of the '67 war was its impact on Jewish young people—the rise of the "Jewish New Left."
Educating children as to the values of Judaism had been difficult in
America, but this war revealed the bankruptcy of the young
people's religious education.

> The reaction of our students to the swastika epi-
> demic and the Eichmann trial [1961] reflected a
> near-complete lack of knowledge of the Nazi pe-
> riod and its effect upon Jewish lives and Jewish life.
> We tend to forget that most Jewish college students
> were infants at the time of Hitler's death; they
> learned nothing, literally nothing, about this trau-
> matic experience in the history of our people. The
> impact of Hitler and of the loss of six million Jews
> to Jewish history is a blank page to them.[22]

Indeed, Jewish young people had a history of being "secularized,"
but now in America there was no closed Jewish community to
which to return. No persecution drove these young people back to

discover their Jewish heritage. Jewish children were badly in need of meaningful Jewish education.

> Having gained the American socio-economic para-
> dise the Jew proceeded to lose his child. Onward
> and upward he had climbed in his quest for the
> material Nirvana. With every difficult step, he had
> jettisoned more of his Jewish baggage, the better to
> be freer and lighter for the drive to the peak. And
> finally, having overcome the obstacles, . . . he
> looked about for his child and heir and found him
> missing. Multiply the scene by its thousands and
> hundred of thousands and the stark picture of as-
> similation and alienation, the most dangerous
> threat to the survival of the Jew as a separate entity,
> comes into focus.[23]

In the areas where the education campaign of the early sixties had failed on Jewish youth, the Six-Day War seemed to accomplish the task in a week of fighting. Before 1967 the young Jewish radicals of the New Left were using the term "genocide" about the American Negroes or North Vietnamese, without recognizing the fact that their own people had been subject, relatively recently, to an effort to kill them all. Now the genocide seemed again to be aimed at them.

Black radical groups came to the fore in the civil rights move-ment and pushed the Jewish leaders aside, labeling them as "ex-ploiters." This viewpoint carried over to the state of Israel, which was seen as an imperialist force in the Middle East:

> All leftist groups seemed to have assumed histori-
> cally that Jewish particularism would have to go.
> Coupled with this everpresent notion is the new
> position of the leftists after the 1967 war, that Israel
> should be condemned as the "Zionist Capitalist
> Nation" and that the Arab Nationalists are the pro-
> letariat to be supported.[24]

Thus Jewish young people banded together as the "Jewish New Left," pitting themselves against the Jewish "establishment," which they saw as a country club institution, not as religious leaders. But more importantly, they did not desire to overthrow Judaism itself, instead they wanted to rediscover and reaffirm their Jewishness.

At last the Jewish people were, as a result of the war, inspired to do things that were "Jewish" as opposed to American: support Israel, learn about Soviet Jewry, and even see the worth of some Jewish customs that their parents had labeled as "not modern." Most important seemed to be the realization that integrating totally into America was not in the best interests of Jewish survival—it would instead be the "royal road to assimilation" and would eventually lead to the demise of American Jewry. No longer was the American way of life a friend, but rather a kind of threat to Jewishness.

> They see American benevolence as distinct a threat
> to Jewish survival as German malevolence was to
> German Jewry. They fear that the grinding down of
> a distinctive Jewish culture is inevitable. They see,
> in other words, that the reverse side of integration
> is cultural and spiritual disintegration.[25]

As far as Jewish identity in America was concerned, the Six-Day War was a help in resurrecting what remained in the American Jewish soul. The Yom Kippur War (1973) served to reinforce its effects, but the problem of identity remains almost schizophrenic. On the one hand is the fear of the loss of Jewishness, and on the other hand is the lure of the secular society—the drive to fit into American culture so completely that all distinctives will be merged into the "ideal American." The problem of assimilation, always present in the American Jewish community, continues to be a large threat to Jewish survival.

America: Graveyard for Jewish Identity?

In order to accurately survey the problem of assimilation which is faced today, it is necessary to hear what Jewish leaders themselves are saying about the problem. First, what is the danger in becoming "truly American"? Surely Jews in other countries have longed to fit into their environment. This certainly cannot be a danger. Not so, say the experts:

Assimilation as the gravedigger of Jewish identity is
not new to history. This lesson was written in blood
for the German Jew. For the American Jew to deny
his Jewish identity is an invitation to a similar disas-
ter no matter how remote it may appear.[26]

The striving to be "enlightened" and become a universalist (sometimes known as "open minded") on the part of American Jewry is
seen as the trend of German Jews also before Hitler.

For a universalist, anti-Semitism isn't an important problem. There are few Jews in the World,
and a universalist will worry about problems of
the many. Yet if you're a Jew, anti-Semitism can
kill you though you're also a universalist. It killed
Jewish universalists on the other side of the ocean
in the other half of the [last] century. If you think
anti-Semitism unworthy of your notice, think
again.[27]

America is not as secure for the Jew as it might seem. It is important to be on guard against anti-Semitism.

Hatred of the Jew exists and is no less today than it
was yesterday. The Jew is not liked in America and
he is not any safer because of his wanting to think
that he is. It is not through education that hatred of
the Jew will be eliminated, for morality and goodness are almost irrelevant to education. [28]

Furthermore, the situation in America is a new one. It is too
comfortable here for many to care about maintaining their cultural
and religious ties.

The argument that Jewry has weathered similar
storms and crises is unwarranted, for never before
have the Jews experienced, over so long and uninter-
rupted a period of time, a way of life which in every

conceivable way militates for assimilation and against the maintenance of a special group identity.[29]

The call of prosperity may be too much for the contemporary American Jew. There is so much to be gained and so little to lose, comparatively.

> The dirty little secret about middle-aged American Jews, especially those on the highest economic levels, is that many dream of being reincarnated as Episcopalians. . . . For most Jews so afflicted actual conversion represents too great a wrench. Many find consolation by fleeing from that which is recognizably Jewish toward such neutral interests as Ethical Culture and Zen Buddhism.[30]

It is no longer the outright threat of conversion to other religions that is foremost, but the idea that a person in America can become secular. Unfortunately, the return to religious commitment on the part of the Jewish New Left has not spread widely enough through the community to forestall the mass migration away from Judaism.

> The era of return to religion has been supplanted by the age of the "death of God" and it is possible to cease being a Jew without having to become anything else. The expectation that these young men and women will eventually return to the Jewish community, as did generations before them and that therefore, we need only sit back and wait, is based on no longer valid assumptions.[31]

No age group is immune from this urge to assimilate. Middle-agers want to fit in with the success-oriented upper middle class. College students are apathetic towards their Jewishness and concentrate more on preparing themselves for future careers. But what are the facts and figures that cause the alarm among Jewish leaders? Is American Jewry dying out? What are the main reasons behind the assimilation?

Facts and Figures

Experts see at least three main causes for assimilation. (Perhaps "assimilation" is not the best term that could be used. What we are examining is a disappearing people.) The first danger of Jewish survival, as has been seen, is the lure of the secular society to the Jew. This pressure is greatest for small-town Jewry—those who do not have large Jewish communities which provide Jewish activities and friends. Statistics show that in Iowa intermarriage is as high as 40%, compared to 20% in large cities like San Francisco and Manhattan.[32] According to a recent survey, only 8% of Jews felt it important to live in accordance with the teachings of their religion, compared with 42% of Catholic respondents and 15% of Protestants.[33]

Intermarriage is the second major danger to survival, and not just in small towns. From 1966 to 1972, 32% of American Jews married Gentiles. A 1974 study showed that 34% of Jewish college graduates intermarried.[34] This problem is very serious to the cause of Jewish survival since the majority of children from these marriages are not given any Jewish education and therefore are lost to the Jewish people. According to the *Jerusalem Post* on May 15, 1997, intermarriage was higher than 50%. The figure in pre-war Germany was 75%.[36] There is the added factor of intermarriage often appearing as a status symbol to Jews with no religious interests:

> Intermarriage presses on the mind of the ambivalent Jew also with forced effectiveness. It is "camp," Jews are told, to choose a non-Jewish spouse. Think of all the jokes made about it, and how popular are Jews who have mixed marriages. Joey Bishop, Jerry Lewis, Jack Klugman, Shecky Green, and a host of others gaudily advertise their mixed marriages . . . Never do they express sympathy for the dismemberment of Jewry.[37]

The third problem is convincing young Jewish married couples to have children, over the cries of groups like "Zero Population Growth" who are urging people to hold the birth rate down. On the average, Jewish couples have 1.5-1.6 children per couple, which is below the replacement level of 2.1.[38] This trend has taken its toll in the lower percentage of Jews in the population of the

United States: in the 1940s, Jews made up approximately 3.5% of the population, while by 1974 the figure was down to 2.8%.[39]

> The problem relates to the failure of young, healthy, gifted, educated, and relatively established Jewish couples to have a sufficient number of children; even on a par with the general population, the fertility rate of which is now at an all-time low. In essence, the American Jewish community is undergoing not zero population growth but the harbinger of virtual zero population.[40]

With the legalization of abortion, the situation is not improving.

Some Implications

Much has been made about the idea that the survival of the Jews this far in history is nothing short of miraculous.

> Other individuals and peoples may wonder how they have come to be what they are; the Jew must wonder why he should exist at all. . . . other peoples require the bond of a common language, or a common land or a common culture in order to continue in existence. The Jew, for long centuries, has had none of these. Consequently, self-appointed experts in the laws of historical change have been quick to predict his impending disappearance. But thus far at least these prophecies have always been confounded. The Jew still exists—a source of wonder both to others and himself.[41]

And the key factor behind this survival has been the staying power of the Jewish faith. So the rise of the "secular society" in America strikes at the heart of this survival.

> . . . To account for Jewish survival is possible only in terms of the Jewish faith. All the other supposed causes of Jewish survival, such as tradition or feelings

of group loyalty, can themselves be explained only in terms of the Jewish faith . . .[42]

If faith itself is being questioned within the Jewish community, then the impetus behind Jewish survival is questioned. American Jews are asking, "Why should I be Jewish?"

> But, if, for purposes of resolving the problematic aspects of being Jewish, one emphasizes those aspects of Jewishness which are most universal, and hence, both least distinctively Jewish and least problematic, what special reason is there to remain a Jew?[43]

Traditional values have been broken down by modern thinkers, but nothing has been presented to take their place.

> What has happened to our young people is that their traditional beliefs in God, in Revelation, in Mitzvah, in Messiah, have been shattered, and they have yet to be replaced by adequate substitutes or up-to-date reinterpretations. Once the validity of these traditional values and convictions have been successfully undermined, the identity of the Jewish student comes seriously into question. There is a definite correlation between loss of faith and attenuation of identity.[44]

Unfortunately, the image of many American synagogues is unattractive to young Jews. Activities of these synagogues seem "clique-ish" and socially irrelevant to the needs of the world.

> What do Jews, particularly young Jews, think about themselves and their fellow Jews? When the word "synagogue" is mentioned, what comes to mind? Empty pews, women with mink coats, card parties, fashion shows, bowling, prayers chanted in a strange and unintelligible language, honors given

only to rich people?—or sincere worship, the study
of an ancient and honored civilization, inspiring
music, moving and informative sermons, commit-
tees involved in social action?[45]

Even the support of Israel and Zionism, once a religious activity,
has moved into the realm of achieving status.

Toward Some Solutions

The lack of a positive image in American Judaism among many
young people offers special challenges for Messianic Judaism. It is
important for Messianic synagogues not to become caught up in
achieving status in exchange for spiritual depth and commitment
to Jewish heritage. A significant area where this must take place is
in children's education. As a new generation of Messianic Jews ar-
rives, we must be prepared to give them a presentation of both the
Messiah and their Jewish heritage that will offer great fulfillment
and involvement as they grow older. Through both the family life
and the synagogue a meaningful purpose for keeping committed to
the faith must be instilled.

It is the *content* of the Messianic Jewish faith which should be
stressed, as opposed to mere emotional appeals. Because of the
Messiah Yeshua (Jesus) and the new life he can give, both in family
life and in congregational life, a dynamic and vital lifestyle can pre-
vail. Messianic Judaism can offer a belief in an active, supernatural
God (unlike other branches of Judaism) and dependence on the
Scriptures which tell of the final victory of Israel. But we must de-
pend on the Scriptures and Spirit of God to lead us, rather than our
great emotional "highs" or a particular leader we like.

At this time there is not much emphasis on those that are
wealthy being leaders in the Messianic Jewish movement, but that
is not to say that it could not become a problem in the future. We
need to be alert.

There are other areas that need to be explored by the Messianic
Jewish movement as it continues to grow: involvement in meaningful social action (traditionally a high point of Judaism); teaching Gentile churches of the dangers of anti-Semitism around the

world; and service to the large percentage of Jewish-Gentile marriages who desire to give their children a "religious" education. These are each challenges to be met and opportunities for witness.

In the long run, however, Messianic Jews can help the survival of the Jewish people most by continuing to remain within the Jewish community, both providing a witness to Yeshua, the Jewish Messiah, and by allowing Jews to remain Jews.

1. *The Jewish Press of Pinellas County*, April 28, 2000. *Jerusalem Report*, January 3, 2000.
2. C. Bezalel Sherman, *The Jew Within American Society* (Detroit: Wayne State University Press, 1961), p. 15.
3. Joseph R. Rosenbloom, "The American Jewish Community," in Belden Menkus, ed., *Meet the American Jew* (Nashville: Broadman Press, 1963), p. 2.
4. Ibid., p. 6. See also "German Immigration and the Shaping of Reform," in Nathan Glazer, *American Judaism*, 2d. ed., rev. (Chicago: University of Chicago Press, 1972), pp. 22–42.
5. Ibid., p. 9.
6. Glazer, *American Judaism*, pp. 77–78.
7. Rosenbloom, "American Jewish Community," p. 11.
8. (New York: Random House, 1968)
9. Arthur Hertzberg, "Zionism," p. 79.
10. Richard Rubenstein, Foreword to *Anti-Semitism and the Christian Mind*, by Alan T. Davies (New York: Herder & Herder, 1969), p. 11.
11. Samuel Sandmel, *The Several Israels* (New York: Ktav Publishing House, 1971) pp. 89.
12. Glazer, *American Judaism*, pp. 108–109.
13. Ibid., p. 115.
14. Ibid., pp. 116–125.
15. Eugene Borowitz, *The Mask Jews Wear* (New York: Simon & Schuster, 1973), p. 45.
16. Irving Greenberg, "Identity in Flux," *Congress Bi-Weekly*, 3 April 1967, p. 10.
17 . Leonard J. Fein, "Modernity and Jewish Identity," *Jewish Digest*, January 1972, p. 40.
18. Greenberg, "Identity," p. 8.
19. Meir Kahane, *Never Again!* (New York: Pyramid Books, 1971) pp. 97.
20. See my thesis, "The Quest for Jewish Survival in America Since 1967 and the Evangelical Community," unpublished master's thesis, Trinity Evangelical Divinity School, June 1976.
21. Norman Podhoretz, "A Certain Anxiety," *Commentary*, August 1971, p. 6.
22. Benjamin Kahn, "Profile of the Young American Jew," *Jewish Digest*, October 1967, p. 26.
23. Kahane, Never Again!, p. 105.

24. Gary A. Glickstein, "Religion and the Jewish New Left," *American Jewish Archives*, 26 (1972): 25.

25. Henry Feingold, "German Jewry Pre-Hitler and American Jewry Today," *Jewish Digest*, January 1972, p. 9.

26. Harold Applebaum, "What Does Jewish Identity Really Mean?" *Reconstructionist*, 7 May 1971, p. 29.

27. Milton Himmelfarb, "Relevance in the Synagogue," *Commentary*, May 1968, p. 43.

28. Kahane, *Never Again!*, pp. 188–89.

29, Marvin Feinstein, "The Menace of Feeling Jewish," *American Zionist*, October 1969, p. 37.

30. Howard Singer, quoted by Jacob Neusner, *American Judaism: Adventure in Modernity* (Englewood Cliffs, N.J.: Prentice-Hall, 1972), p. 81.

31. Leon A. Jick, "American Jewry: Community and Campus," *Jewish Frontier*, February 1969, p. 10.

32. Harold Goldmeier, "Vanishing American Jewry?" *Congress Bi-Weekly*, 21 June 1974, p. 11.

33. Benjamin Kahn, "Profile of the Young American Jew," *Jewish Digest*, October 1967, p. 23.

34. Milton Himmelfarb, "No Jews, No Jewish Identity," *Jewish Digest*, October 1974, p. 18.

35. Goldmeier, "Vanishing?," p. 11.

36. Robert Gordis, *Judaism in a Christian World*, (New York: McGraw-Hill Book Co., 1966) p. 186.

37. Goldmeier, "Vanishing?," p. 11.

38. *Jerusalem Post*, May 15, 1997.

39. Himmelfarb, "No Jews," p. 18.

40. Roberts, "Jewish Genocide?," p. 37.

41. Emil Fackenheim, *Quest for Past and Future*, (Bloomington: Indiana University Press. 1968). p. 112.

42. Ibid., p. 114.

43. Fein, "Modernity," p. 38.

44. Kahn, "Profile," p. 23.

45. "The Image of Jews in the Minds of American Jews," *Reconstructionist*, December 1966, p. 5.

THE PLACE OF RABBINIC TRADITION IN A MESSIANIC JEWISH LIFESTYLE

John Fischer

It is not uncommon in Messianic circles of varying perspectives to encounter definite apathy or even strong hostility toward the traditions of our people and to "the Rabbis" presumably responsible for them. So, "Rabbinic Judaism," and all it has espoused, is often presented by these critics as a vicious enemy to Messianic Judaism, completely devoid of anything beneficial. And the Oral Torah—the basis for our traditions—is frequently pictured as diametrically opposed to God's "true Torah."

Sadly, many of those who attack "the Rabbis" have never read them, let alone can they name more than one or two! Is this kind of vehement attack the best approach to relating to the rabbis, to the Oral Torah and our traditions, and to "Rabbinic Judaism"? And is this the only way to respond to "the Rabbis"? I would like to suggest another.

Yeshua and the Traditions

Several examples from Yeshua's life illustrate his approach to the traditions. A very significant passage is Luke 4:15f. Here, Yeshua attends a synagogue, participates in its service, and reads the Haftarah portion (the Scripture reading from the Prophets) of the day.

Much of the traditional synagogue service was already intact during Yeshua's time, as the Dead Sea Scrolls confirm. Fragments of scrolls of both daily and festival prayers dating to the Hasmonean period (first to second century B.C.E.) from the fourth cave at Qumran show striking parallels to the traditional prayers in content, structure and texts. Since the prayers in these scrolls exhibit nothing sectarian—unlike the other documents which contain specific

Qumran terminology and ideas—these prayers were part of the broader Jewish community. These findings lend support to the tradition that the men of the Great Assembly, reaching back approximately to Ezra's time, established the basic structure of the synagogue service followed to this day.[1]

The synagogue, its service, and the cycle of readings are all "traditional" institutions, in which Yeshua approvingly participated. And his followers shared the same attachment to these traditional institutions. For example, there is strong evidence to suggest that the gospels are structured as a commentary on the cycle of Jewish lexical and holiday readings.[2]

The Gospels also indicate Yeshua's use of prayers and blessings from the *siddur* (prayerbook), another product of the "traditions." The "Lord's Prayer" of Matthew 6 reflects the third, fifth, sixth and ninth benedictions of the *'Amidah* (the central prayer of the synagogue service).[3] In Luke 22:19 and following, Yeshua utilized the traditional blessings over the bread.

Of his life as a whole, two passages are most characteristic and instructive. In the first situation, Yeshua challenges the crowds, which include the religious leaders, "Who among you can accuse me of any wrong?" (John 8:46) No one comes forward to claim he had violated any of the biblical laws or any of the Jewish traditions. Not one religious leader is able to point to a flaw in his behavior or conduct even with respect to the traditions! The same holds true in the second situation. Yeshua stands before the Sanhedrin (Mark 14:55–56). Some of the religious leaders try to find something of which to accuse him. Nevertheless, they are unable to find one thing in his life that they can present as a violation; he had lived flawlessly according to the traditions. Finally, they find something. As a man he had claimed to be God—blasphemy from their perspective. They can accuse him of no other violation of the Law or the traditions!

Yeshua's teachings show the same consistency with the traditions as his life does. A crucial passage in this respect is Matt. 5:17–19 and its context. Here Yeshua states that he has "not come to abolish the Law and the Prophets but to fulfill them." He then repeats this claim to reinforce his statement. The thrust of the terms he uses is significant. The term "abolish" (*kataluo*) means "to do away with, abolish, annul, make invalid, repeal." And he twice says he will not do anything of this kind. Quite the contrary, as the Greek construction here (*ouk . . . alla*) indicates, he has come to fulfill, "fulfill" being the direct opposite of "abolish." In other words, everything "abolish" is, "fulfill" is not: the two cannot simultaneously describe the same situation. The term "fulfill" (*pleroo*) carries with it the idea of "cram full, make complete; fill out; confirm; show forth the true, full meaning; bring to full expression";[4] or, as the English intimates, "fill full."

The linguistic background of Yeshua sheds further light on his statements. The native languages of Yeshua and his hearers were Hebrew and Aramaic. Therefore, Matthew's account here is a translation of what Yeshua said. The Aramaic for "fulfill" (*la'asuphe*) means "to add," with the connotation "to preserve the intended meaning by including all the actions implied in the statement." And this is precisely what Yeshua does beginning at 5:20; he includes all the actions implicit in the commands of God. The Hebrew equivalent (*kiyyem*) means "to uphold" with the sense that "the teaching given agrees with the text of the Scripture in question."

The very formula Yeshua uses from 5:20 on—a formula so often very wrongly interpreted and, therefore, badly distorted—picks up this same emphasis, namely, that the interpretation given agrees with the Scripture text. The formula, "You have heard . . . but I say," is built on a common rabbinic formula[5] which does not mean to set aside the biblical text, but rather, to give the correct, complete interpretation which truly upholds the biblical text. Even the very terms "fulfill" and "destroy" are part of the rabbinic discussions.[6] He was not setting aside, he was filling out; he was not contrasting, he was complementing. It is true that Yeshua's statements here refer primarily to the text of Scripture. However, in the period of Second Temple Judaism, there was already developing a series of interpretations and applications associated with the Scripture texts, and these were very definitely part of the background of the texts, and were, in fact, incorporated into his interpretation of the texts.[7] So, to paraphrase Yeshua at this point, he said: "Not only do I not overthrow the Law and the traditions, or empty them of their content; on the contrary, I fill them full to the brim."

This perspective of Yeshua's is further reinforced by his statements in Matt. 23:2–3, where he instructs his followers, "Whatever the Pharisees teach, that do." Since the Pharisees and their allies were the religious traditionalists and proto-rabbis of the first century, Yeshua's instruction certainly encompasses the "rabbinic traditions" of his day. In fact, many of the traditions, or *halakhot* (as they were already called in the Hasmonean period), were definitely in place during the Second Temple period. As Professor Lawrence Schiffman notes, based on the evidence from the Dead Sea Scrolls:

> The Talmudic materials are far more accurate than previously thought . . . the terminology, and even some of the very laws as recorded in rabbinic sources (some in the name of the Pharisees, and others attributed to anonymous first-century sages), were actually used and espoused by the Pharisees. In other words—and this is extremely important—Rabbinic Judaism as embodied in the Talmud is not a post-destruction invention, as some scholars had maintained; on the contrary, the roots of Rabbinic Judaism reach back at least to the Hasmonean period.[8]

Upon further reflection, these results should not be that surprising. After all, Gerhardsson[9] has shown for the New Testament, the oral transmission of both narrative and didactic materials over many years can be completely trustworthy and historically accurate. And this is particularly true when dealing with societies such as that of Second Temple Judaism—whose educational system is orally oriented.[10] In his anthropological study of orally oriented societies, Ong[11] has described and demonstrated how verbal accounts and historical events are *accurately* transmitted orally over many generations (which is precisely the situation for the rabbinic sources). It would, therefore, be appropriate to conclude that:

> We now know . . . that oral tradition in pre-Talmudic Jewish sources are often extraordinarily accurate even as far back as the Exilic period or earlier. The data contained in our rabbinic sources of the second century A.D. and later are proving reliable for earlier times than generally believed. The sayings of the leading Jewish teachers of the intertestamental

and NT periods were preserved with remarkable tenacity for centuries after their original date.[12]

In light of this and of Matthew 23 it is not surprising to find virtually all of Yeshua's teachings, from the Sermon on the Mount on, paralleled in the rabbinic materials.[13] Several examples should suffice at this point.

> He who is merciful to others shall receive mercy from Heaven. (Shab. 151b; cf. Matt. 5:7)

> Let your yes be yes and your no be no. (Baba Metzia 49a; cf. Matt. 5:37)

> Do they say, "Take the splinter out of your eye"? He will retort, "Remove the beam out of your own eye." (Baba Bathra 15b; cf. Matt. 7:3)

But didn't Yeshua condemn the Pharisees? Yes, he did in Matthew 23, but for their hypocrisy, not for their teachings. And it's at the beginning of this chapter that he urged his followers to follow their teachings (vv. 2–3). His criticism is no more severe than the Pharisees' own criticism of themselves in the Talmud. Here they call the hypocrites and insincere among themselves "sore spots" and "plagues" and "destroyers of the world" (Ber. 14b; Hag. 14a; Sotah 3.4). Their main concern, as it was for Yeshua, was hypocrisy and lack of sincerity.

On occasion, Yeshua's attitude to Shabbat appears lax (Mark 2:23–28; Matt. 12:1–8). The religious leaders had criticized Yeshua for his disciples' actions in picking grain on Shabbat. Yeshua's response is often presented as evidence that he disregarded the regulations for Shabbat observance. However, at this time in history, there was an ongoing discussion over the picking and eating of grain on Shabbat. Even the Talmud points out: "Bundles which can be taken up with one hand may be handled on the Sabbath . . . and he may break it with his hand and eat thereof" (Shab. 128a). This is exactly what the disciples were doing. Further, Yeshua's reasoning concerning his position on this issue follows the same patterns used by the Pharisees to demonstrate that the needs of life are

paramount, even over the Sabbath regulations. Both cite Hosea
6:6 (Matt. 12:7; Suk. 49b), David eating the Tabernacle bread,
and the Sabbath sacrifices at the Temple to make their point.[14]
Even Yeshua's concluding statement is found in the Talmud: "Sabbath was made for man, not man for the Sabbath" (Mark 2:27;
Yoma 85b). In neither case are the Sabbath regulations being set
aside.

A similar kind of problem arises with respect to Yeshua's statements about eating and washing (Matt. 15:1–8; Mark 7:1–19).
Here Yeshua enters into the handwashing discussion going on between the Pharisaic Schools of Hillel and Shammai.[15] Some Pharisees opted for stricter rules of cleanliness than others. Yeshua makes
some comments about ritual cleanness and internal corruption and
discusses what constitutes real cleanness and uncleanness. His approach is paralleled in the rabbinic materials.[16] Then he makes the
statement that is usually translated: "Thus he declared all foods
clean" (Mark 7:19). Based on this passage, some say he abolished
kashrut, the dietary laws. However, that would be inconsistent
with his argument earlier, where he warns some of the Pharisees
against invalidating God's laws by inappropriate traditions. If he
here invalidates God's kosher laws, Yeshua contradicts himself!
Years later, Shim'on sees a sheet descending from heaven and is
given the instruction to kill and eat all the animals on the sheet.
Neither the voice from the Lord nor Shim'on ever mentions
Yeshua's supposed abolishing of *kashrut*, as would be expected in
this situation had Yeshua actually set aside the kosher laws. The
only application Scripture makes of the vision is that Shim'on
should talk to Cornelius (Acts 10 and 11), not that *kashrut* has
been set aside.

A comparison with the Greek of Mark 7:19 points to a solution. The "cleansing" referred to by Yeshua here is grammatically
related to the "latrine," not to the food![17] In other words, Yeshua
said, as the KJV correctly translates here, "Because it enters not
into his heart but into his belly and then goes out into the latrine,
thus purging (or eliminating) all food." Yeshua used the process of
digestion and elimination to reinforce his point that inner cleanliness must accompany outer cleanliness to be effective. He was not
even referring to *kashrut*, let alone abolishing it!

Others question the propriety, rabbinically, of Yeshua's healing
on the Sabbath. However, rabbinic rulings of his day would allow

his Sabbath healings. Safrai concludes: "Jesus' Sabbath healings which angered the head of the synagogue were permitted by tannaitic law."[18]

After reviewing Yeshua's relationship to the Judaism of his day, it would not be inappropriate to describe Yeshua as a Pharisee in good standing.[19] This may sound like heresy to some people. However, contrary to what many may think, the Pharisees as a whole were not anxious seekers of merit before God to gain themselves a place in heaven. As noted evangelical scholar Donald Hagner, among numerous others, has pointed out, the Pharisees had a definite understanding of the grace of God and a solid grasp of the Scriptures.[20] They had a profound concern for piety and purity, and for a proper heart attitude toward God.[21] The New Testament criticism is directed at only a few among them. So appropriately, Orthodox Israeli scholar and rabbi Pinhas Lapide described Yeshua as a traditional, observant Jew:

> Jesus never and no where broke the law of Moses, nor did he in any way provoke its infringement—it is entirely false to say that he did. . . . In this respect you must believe me, for I do know my Talmud more or less. . . . This Jesus was as faithful to the law as I would hope to be. But I suspect that Jesus was more faithful to the law than I am—and I am an Orthodox Jew.[22]

To this may be appended the evaluation of historian and rabbi Joseph Klausner: "Despite all the Christian antagonism to the Pharisees, the teaching of the Pharisees remained the basis of Christian teaching."[23] Quite clearly, Yeshua remained an observant, traditional Jew, both in his life and in his teachings.

Rav Sha'ul and the Traditions

In his life, the great rabbi from Tarsus, Rav Sha'ul, reflects the same respect for the traditions. In Acts 13:15 he is invited to speak in the synagogue because he is recognized as a religious leader or teacher by his dress, a matter of tradition.[24] In Acts 23:6 he claims, "I am a Pharisee," not "I was a Pharisee." Then in Acts 26:5 he adds, "They have known me for a long time and can testify that according to the strictest sect of our religion I have lived as a Pharisee." The Greek tense here indicates not only past behavior but a continuing life-style. On his arrival in Rome, Rav Sha'ul confirms his attitude to-ward the traditions. He explains his situation to the leaders of the Jewish community in Rome and defends himself (Acts 28:17): "I have not violated the customs (or traditions) of our fathers." In other words, he has faithfully followed Yeshua's instructions about observing the teachings of the Pharisees (Matt. 23:2–3).

His teachings are consistent with his life-style, as Romans 3:31 indicates: "Does faith nullify the law. No! It upholds it!" (cf. Matt. 5:17) That his teachings reflect his observant attitude is also clearly demonstrated in his discussion with Ya'akov, Yeshua's brother (Acts 21:20f). They meet on Rav Sha'ul's return to Jerusalem, and Ya'akov tells him of a rumor circulating about him, that Rav Sha'ul is teaching Jews "not to live according to our traditions." In order to counter this rumor, Ya'akov suggests a demonstration of his commitment to the traditions. "Take to the Temple this group of Messianic Jewish men who have made a religious vow, join their purification rites and pay their expenses." Then, as he says, "Every-one will know that there is no truth to the reports about you." Rav Sha'ul follows this excellent suggestion so that those "zealous for the law" can rest assured of his commitment to the traditions both in his life and in his teaching.[25]

But doesn't Galatians contradict the previous analysis? Doesn't Rav Sha'ul teach here that grace is opposed to the traditions? Not in any way![26] In fact, he declares: "The law is not opposed to the promises [or grace] of God!" (3:21) Moreover, the term "law," which he uses frequently in his letters, can refer to anything from Scripture to laws in general to legalism; it has a multiplicity of uses. In fact, Rav Sha'ul refers to six different kinds of "law" in Romans 7 alone! In Galatians he focuses his attack on legalism. There, the terms are parallel to the concepts of flesh, works and self-effort. Therefore, he is attacking not the traditions, but the idea that a person's efforts and achievements earn that person merit (or stand-ing) before God. As noted Jewish scholar H.J. Schoeps observed:

> Paul may well be conducting a justifiable polemic
> against the erroneous opinions of this or that
> scholar among his . . . opponents. But he is not say-

ing anything contrary to Holy Scripture [which doesn't teach that] the law gives justificationary merit.[27]

To this, the noted Christian scholar R. Alan Cole adds:

> Paul never seems to have compelled the Gentile Churches to act like Jews . . . but it remains equally true that he does not expect Jewish Churches to act like Gentile believers. He never says that it is wrong for them to be circumcised, or to keep the law, or to observe the festivals. All he insists is that these have nothing to do with the gift of salvation.[28]

Some among the first-century Jewish people had missed the message of the Torah and the significance of the traditions. They distorted and transformed their observance into works, self-effort and self-achievement, into a means of getting right with God by one's own strength and merit; i.e. legalism. They taught Gentile believers that self-effort and works (doing certain things) resulted in salvation and/or spirituality (3:3; 5:4). This, and not the traditions, Rav Sha'ul vigorously attacked.

However, his attack against legalism must not be misconstrued. H.L. Ellison reminds us:

> We are justified in thinking that throughout his missionary activity Paul lived in a way that would have called forth no adverse comment from a Pharisee who might have met him.[29]

Throughout his life, Rav Sha'ul remained a consistent, observant Pharisee (Acts 26:5; 28:17).

The Sh'lichim and the Traditions

Yeshua's stance and Rav Sha'ul's observance find both biblical and historical corroboration in the practices of the Sh'lichim (apostles). The first-century Jewish historian Josephus records the martyrdom of Yeshua's brother Ya'akov (Antiquities xx.9.1). Ya'akov aroused the ire of the religious leadership, so they had him thrown over the Temple wall. The Pharisees were so incensed—because of their respect for Ya'akov and his devout, observant life—that they sent a delegation to Rome and demanded the removal of the High Priest! Ya'akov was not alone in living as a consistent, traditional Jew, a "tzaddik," as he was described by his contemporaries.[30]

Irenaeus, a second-century leader whose teacher was taught by the Sh'lichim, and who therefore had accurate knowledge of their lives, wrote concerning the Sh'lichim (*Against Heresies* 3.23.15): "But they themselves . . . continued in the ancient observances. . . . Thus did the apostles . . . scrupulously act according to the dispensation of the Mosaic law." In other words, the Sh'lichim carefully followed Yeshua's instructions to observe the traditions (Matt. 23:2–3).

The apostles remained fully involved in the Jewish community. They continued to worship in the Temple (Acts 2:46; 3:1). They continued to worship in the synagogue and to pray the liturgy (Acts 2:42, where "to prayer" literally reads "to the prayers"). "The prayers" describe the set prayers of the synagogue liturgy. In fact, there is some evidence that Shim'on actually wrote a bit of the synagogue liturgy, specifically one of the Shabbat prayers, a poetic section of the Yom Kippur liturgy, and more.[31] Considering this, it is no wonder that several centuries later believers were still following the apostolic practice of observing the traditions, as Epiphanius notes (c. 400 C.E.) about the Nazarenes (Panarion xxx, 18; xxxix, 7):

> They are mainly Jews and nothing else. They make use not only of the New Testament, but they also use in a way the Old Testament of the Jews; for they do not forbid the books of the Law, the Prophets, and the Writings . . . so that they are approved of by the Jews, from whom the Nazarenes do not differ in anything and they profess all the dogmas pertaining to the prescriptions of the Law and to the customs of the Jews, except they believe in Christ. . . . They teach that there is but one God, and his son [Yeshua HaMashiach]. But they are well learned in the Hebrew language; for they, like the Jews, read the whole Law, then the Prophets [i.e., they use the

> cycle of synagogue Scripture readings]. . . . They
> differ from the Jews because they believe in Mes-
> siah, and from the Christians in that they are to this
> day bound to the Jewish rites, such as circumcision,
> the Sabbath, and other ceremonies.

Often, however, the "addition" of the twelfth benediction (against the *minim*) to the *'Amidah* is presented as evidence that the early Messianic Jews no longer remained a part of the Jewish community and therefore severed themselves from the traditions. This position argues that "the Rabbis" added the twelfth benediction to the existing eighteen of the *'Amidah*, giving the *'Amidah* its now-traditional form of nineteen benedictions. The twelfth, the argument continues, with its condemnation of the *minim* (heretics) was aimed at ostracizing and isolating the early Messianic Jews.

Three major historical roadblocks stand as obstacles to this position. The first is the evidence of Shim'on's contributions to the liturgy. The second is the previously-quoted description of the Nazarenes by Epiphanius as "approved of by the Jews." Neither of these fits the *minim* scenario. Then third, there is the history of the *'Amidah* itself. The fifteenth benediction ("make flourish the offspring of David . . . make flourish the horn of salvation") was not yet recited in Israel as late as the seventh century. It is, therefore, the later addition; the twelfth isn't. This is corroborated by the traditional siddur. There are Purim additions in the form of poems (*piyyutim*) for every one of the benedictions except the fifteenth. These poetic additions were composed by Eleazar HaKallir (c. 77 C.E.). Evidently HaKallir did not have the Fifteenth benediction in front of him when he wrote his poems. The benediction that was added to the eighteen was therefore the fifteenth, not the twelfth (the *minim*).[32] In addition, later some synagogues added to their curse against the *minim* the term *notzrim* (Nazarenes), further indicating that "against the *minim*" was neither added nor did it particularly focus on Messianic Jews.[33] The Oxford Jewish scholar Vermes points out:

> In fact, in the late nineteenth and early twentieth
> century most experts tend to regard "Minim" as
> the rabbinic name for that [Messianic Jewish]

> community. . . . But although M. Simon has re-
> cently shown that Christians were referred to as
> Minim in the fourth century, the title barely fits
> the Judeo-Christians of the apostolic and sub-ap-
> ostolic age.[34]

Reflecting on the first century, Jewish scholar Isidore Epstein accurately described the apostolic and early Messianic Jewish practice:

> The earliest adherents . . . regarded Jesus as the
> Messiah. They make no other changes. They con-
> tinued to go to the Temple, and presumably to the
> synagogue, as they had been accustomed to do . . .
> they conformed in every respect to the usual Jewish
> observances.[35]

Quite clearly the Sh'lichim remained a part of the "traditional" Jewish community.

This biblical pattern emerges: Yeshua, Rav Sha'ul, the Sh'lichim, and the early Messianic Jews all deeply respected the traditions and devoutly observed them, and in so doing, set a useful pattern for us to follow. However, several underlying assumptions or operational principles need to be spelled out. Above all, the traditions are not authoritative for Messianic Jews—only the Bible has that role. Anything that contradicts Scripture does not belong in Messianic Judaism. However, the traditions are usually beneficial and elevating. Messianic Jews can learn and appreciate much through them. Not that the traditions have no shortcomings, but they possess a great deal of richness, beauty and depth.

The Holidays

If we did not have the traditions to fill out the details of the biblical holiday instructions, our observance would lose significant dimension and depth, and our celebrations would be correspondingly diminished.

The traditions have provided us with the Pesach *haggadah* (the guide to the ceremony of the Passover), setting forth the order and elements of the seder (Passover meal). The stirring images and striking pictures which richly reflect Yeshua would be lost to us apart from the "traditional" seder. The traditions give us the *afikomen* (the broken matzah used for dessert) and the three pieces of matzah, the cup of redemption, Elijah's cup, and more.

Without the traditions, we would not know that Shavu'ot (Pentecost) is more than a harvest festival, that it celebrates the giving of the Torah and the formalizing of God's covenant with us. We would then miss the impact of the work of the Ruach HaShem (Spirit of God) at the Shavu'ot of Acts 2, where he writes the Torah on hearts, and renews his covenant with his people (Jer. 31:31f.). The traditions also speak of the Moroccan Jewish custom of pouring large containers of water over the Shavu'ot celebrants to picture the prophecy of Ezekiel concerning the coming of the Spirit (36:25–27).

The traditions remind us that Rosh HaShanah is more then just the Festival of Trumpets. It celebrates the creation of the world. And "the Rabbis" remind us that the sounding of the shofar will announce the Messiah's coming and will usher in the Messianic age, the time of the world's recreation. The traditions give us the ceremony of *tashlikh*, with its reminder that Mic. 7:18–20 is the basis for participating in the Messianic age and the new creation.[36] "The Rabbis" wrote the striking prayer at the blowing of the shofar which mentions Yeshua as "the Prince of God's Presence."[37]

The Yom Kippur liturgy provides us with *'Az Milifney B'rey'shit*, the startling *musaf* prayer which describes the Messiah in terms from Isaiah 53 and requests his return to his people. The liturgy also paints the pictures of Messiah's death and resurrection by means of its stress on the "sacrifice" of Isaac and the reading of the book of Jonah. And the traditions keep alive the basic message of atonement by sacrifice through the custom of *kapparot*.[38]

The historical customs surrounding Sukkot (Tabernacles) gave Yeshua the perfect opportunity to present himself as the source of living water (John 7) and as the light of the world (John 8) against the stirring backdrop of the Temple water-drawing ceremony and the lighting of the Temple courtyard menorah.[39] The existing traditions of the waving of the *lulav* remind us of Yeshua's last entry into Jerusalem (Matt. 21:1–9) and anticipate his return through the Golden Gate. Finally, the accompanying *Hosha'not* prayers and the traditionally prescribed reading from Zechariah 14 both beautifully picture the time of his coming.

The ancient traditions add so much to our celebration and enjoyment of the holidays! We would lose much by way of insights and joy had they not filled out the details of the biblical instructions.

The Liturgy

The traditional liturgy, besides that which relates to the holidays, provides us with awesome and inspiring reflections of God as well as breathtaking opportunities and vehicles to worship him.

The words of the special *kaddish* chanted as part of the burial service ring out with stirring hope:

> May his great name be magnified and sanctified in the world that he will create anew, when he will raise the dead, and give them eternal life; will rebuild the city of Jerusalem, and establish his Temple in the middle of it; and will uproot all pagan worship from the earth, and restore the worship of the true God. O may the Holy One, blessed be he, reign in his sovereignty and majesty during your lifetime, and during the lifetime of all the house of Israel, speedily, soon, and say, Amen.
>
> Let his great name be blessed forever and for all eternity.
>
> Blessed, praised and glorified, exalted, extolled and honored, magnified and lauded be the name of the Holy One, blessed be he, though he transcends all blessings and hymns, praises and songs, which are uttered in the world; and say, Amen.
>
> May there be great peace from heaven, and life for us and for all Israel; and say, Amen.
>
> He who makes peace in his heavenly realms, may he make peace for us and for all Israel; and say, Amen.[40]

Then there is the rich beauty of the words beginning *Nishmat kol-chai*, which elevate participants to the heights of worship:

> Every living thing shall bless Your name, O Lord
> our God, and all flesh shall ever acclaim and exalt
> your fame, O our King. From everlasting to ever-
> lasting you are God; and beside you we have no
> King, who redeems and saves, liberates and deliv-
> ers, who supports and comforts in all times of
> trouble and distress; yes, we have no King but you.
>
> You are the God of the first and of the last ages,
> God of all creatures, Lord of all generations,
> adored in countless praises, guiding your world
> with faithful love and your creatures with tender
> mercies . . . he makes the dumb to speak, liberates
> the prisoners, supports the falling, and raises up
> those who are bowed down.
>
> To you alone we give thanks. Were our mouths
> full of songs as the sea, and our tongues full of
> praise as its many waves, and our lips full of thanks
> as the wide expanse of the skies: were our eyes shin-
> ing with light like the sun and the moon, and our
> hands were spread forth like the wings of eagles,
> and feet were swift as the wild deer, we would still
> be unable to thank you and praise your name, O
> Lord our God and God of our fathers, for one
> thousandth or one ten thousandth part of the
> bounties which you have bestowed on our fathers
> and on us . . . may your name be exalted, our King,
> forever and throughout all generations.[41]

The liturgy also invites us to come before God in repentance, expecting him to respond because of his grace. So the sixth bene-diction of the daily *'Amidah* expects us to pray: "Forgive us, our Father, for we have sinned; pardon us, our King, for we have trans-gressed, for you pardon and forgive. Blessed are you, O Lord, gra-cious and ever ready to forgive."

In fact, a major portion of the liturgy teaches or describes God's grace. During *Shacharit* (the daily morning prayers) we pray: "Sovereign of all worlds! Not because of our righteous acts do we lay our supplications before you, but because of your abun-dant mercies." During *Minchah* (the daily afternoon service) we add: "Our Father, our King, be gracious to us and answer us, for we have no good works of our own; deal with us in graciousness and loving kindness, and save us." Finally, during *Ma'ariv* (the evening service), we include Psalm 51, which so clearly expresses our need to rely on God, not on ourselves, because we are sinners.

In their discussions and commentaries, "the Rabbis" repeatedly refer to God's graciousness. For example, in the *Midrashim* they reflect:

> "Deal with your servant according to your grace" (Ps. 119:124). Perhaps you take pleasure in our good works? Merit and good works we have not; act toward us in grace (Tehillim Rabbah, on 119:123).

Statements such as this prompted C.G. Montefiore to comment about "the Rabbis'" perspective: "One might almost say that man was created in order to give opportunity for God to display His forgiveness, His loving kindness, His mercy, His grace."[42]

His remarks form part of a very extensive selection of passages on God's grace drawn from the rabbinic sources.

Montefiore did accurately assess the importance of God's graciousness in the rabbinic materials: it is a significant and representative aspect of "the Rabbis'" thinking, not an isolated stream. Orthodox scholar Lapide makes this quite clear: "It is evident to all Masters of the Talmud that salvation, or participation in the coming world, as it is called in Hebrew, can be attained only through God's gracious love [grace]."[43] The evangelical scholar William Sanford La Sor also attested to this.

> Salvation is always and everywhere in Scripture by the grace of God. There is no other way of salvation in either the Old Testament or the New. A study of the Jewish Prayer Book will show that this is also the faith of the Jews.[44]

However, much misinformation persists to the effect that Judaism is a religion of law and Christianity is a religion of grace. To help set the record straight, Dr. James Sanders, President of the

Ancient Biblical Manuscript Center in Claremont, California, addressed these remarks to the 1988 graduating class of Hebrew Union College:

> To say that grace supersedes law is totally to misunderstand Torah. Torah was and is a gift of God's grace (e.g., Deut. 7:6–8). God did not just liberate us and leave us on our own. God immediately thereon made justice the line and righteousness the plummet. God gave our ancestors not only the Torah, but also his own spirit (e.g., Num. 11:29). The gospels clarify that Jesus himself was for observant Jews in his day more stringent (e.g., Matt. 19:21–2) in interpreting Torah and laws related to it than either of the Pharisaic houses, and even more perhaps than the authors of the Dead Sea Scrolls, as Yigael Yadin used to say. I do not think that Paul was in any way pitting faith against works. What he asked quite clearly was in whose works should we have faith, God's or ours (e.g., Rom. 10:1–4)? And no rabbi has ever said, to my knowledge, that a Jew should have faith in human works and not in God's works.[45]

In addition, "the Rabbis" even had a concept of vicarious atonement, one person dying in the place of another to secure his atonement.[46] And, of course, the Talmud reminds us: "Does not atonement come through the blood, as it is said: 'For it is the blood that makes an atonement by reason of the life'?" (Yoma 5a)

The ancient, traditional Jewish penitential prayer, the Prayer of Manasseh, beautifully presents the issues involved in having a relationship with God.

> (11) And now behold I am bending the knees of my heart before you; and I am beseeching your kindness. (12) I have sinned, O Lord, I have sinned; and I certainly know my sins. (13) I beseech you; forgive me! Do not destroy me with my transgressions; do not be angry against me forever;

do not remember my evils; and do not condemn me and banish me to the depths of the earth! For you are the God of those who repent. (14) In me you will manifest all your grace; and although I am not worthy, you will save me according to your manifold mercies. (15) Because of this (salvation) I shall praise you continually all the days of my life; because all the host of heaven praise you, and sing to you forever and ever.[47]

To this, only one more thing needs to be added, the statement of the Talmud: ". . . then came the prophet Habakkuk and reduced all the commands to one, as it is written: 'the just shall live by his faith.'" (Makkot 23–24)

Understanding the Traditions

But there is still other misinformation that needs correcting. Some people think that "the Rabbis" revere the Oral Law more than they respect the Scriptures. However, no rabbi should imply that the Oral Law is equal to or on a par with the biblical text. As a prominent modern rabbi pointed out:

> After the weekly reading of the prophetic portion in the synagogue, the reader concludes with a blessing that praises God "all of whose words are true and just" and "who is faithful to all of his words." In so doing, the reader expresses the conviction that the text he has just read is the Word of God. No such blessing is conceivable over a rabbinic text.
>
> The biblical text is unique as the Word of God. The oral law elaborates and interprets the scriptural text in such a way that in spite of all the importance Judaism attaches to the oral law, it does not eclipse the primacy of the Bible as the Word of God.[48]

The concept of "the chosen people" or "the election of Israel" poses a problem for some people. In fact, the misinformed, as well as many anti-Semites, accuse "the Rabbis" of using this concept to teach the superiority and exclusivity of the Jewish people. Nothing could be farther from the truth! "The Rabbis" teach that:

> We believe that the nations and peoples of the world have their Divine purposes and their assigned roles to fulfill, too, for God is the God of all the world, not just of Jewry. And we see our divinely ordained assignment as involving a unique role, one to which history itself bears witness. It implies a special purpose in life, a reason for our existence. That purpose is not to make Jews of all the world, but to bring the peoples of all the world, whatever their distinctive beliefs may be, to an acknowledgment of the sovereignty of God and to an acceptance of the basic values revealed to us by that God. It is to serve as a means by which blessing will be brought to "all the families of the earth" (Gen. 12:3).
>
> It is this mission which underlies for Jews the coming of the day "when all mankind will call upon Thy name." It is only in these terms, supernatural though they may be, that any plausible explanation can be offered for Israel's ability to survive against the many obstacles and threats to its very existence. . . . It is in these terms that we discover meaning even in Israel's historical suffering and dispersion, as in its achievements, its strengths, and its restoration to Zion.[49]

This analysis is completely in accord with the teachings of Scripture (Exod. 19:5–6; Deut. 4:5–8; Isa. 42:6; Rom. 9:45).

Misunderstanding the Traditions

Some people have declared that the siddur is devoid of truth. On the contrary, the siddur overflows with biblical statements and sentiments, as the earlier discussion indicated and as Messianic Jewish scholar Rachmiel Frydland documented in his many articles. Well over 90% of the siddur incorporates direct quotations of Scripture.

And much of the remainder involves mosaics of Bible verses or phrases of Scripture. Even the sections of "original" prayer, though rare, abound in biblical allusions. To the foregoing assessment, Miller[50] adds this further insightful analysis.

> For us to pray in English implies an acceptance of the value system reflected by the English language! So also it is with Hebrew and its reflection of the biblical value system and outlook. In a sense, no language is totally transparent; it is ideological, i.e., "the medium is the message."

Finally, the traditional prayers, if rightly understood, serve as motivators and inspirers of real worship, not as inhibitors![51]

Does utilizing the traditions violate the biblical command "to go outside the camp" (Heb. 13:13), as some have charged? If this passage is interpreted correctly by keeping it in its context, absolutely not! The phrase "outside the camp" comes from Exod. 33:7 and Num. 19:9. The "Tent of Meeting" originally stood "outside the camp." Here God met with Moses (Exod. 33:8–11). People came here to be cleansed by the ashes of the red heifer (Num. 19:9). The bodies of the animals used in the Yom Kippur sacrifices were burned here, and the scapegoat was released here (Lev. 16:20–27). This place "outside the camp" stood not as something distinct from Judaism, but served as the center and focus of early Jewish faith and as the place of communicating with God! Appropriately, Yeshua died here, as Hebrews describes it, in fulfillment of the images and lessons of the sacrifice system and consistent with, not in contrast to, Jewish religion. The readers of Hebrews understood the command to "go outside the camp" as a challenge to return to God and identify with Judaism as properly centered, centered in Yeshua, who makes all the traditions come alive. This was not a command to withdraw from the traditions and practices, but a challenge to return and observe them properly, in light of Yeshua, the true—not the new—center of Judaism. God wanted them to return to the true center and practice of their faith—in the spirit of Isa. 2:2–3—not to withdraw from the traditions.[52]

Further, others claim that "Rabbinic" Judaism is a Babylonian religion that is ungodly and man-made. This view is based on the notion that since the Talmud originated in Babylon, it absorbed into itself an alien religion. There are a number of major flaws in this line of reasoning because it ignores (or is unaware of) history. Judah HaNasi compiled the *Mishnah*, the central core of the Talmud. The *Beyt Din* he presided over was located at Tiberias and then Sepphoris, not in Babylon. Judah's work was based on that of Rabbis Akiva and Meir, both of Israel, which in turn was based on the *halakhot* of earlier Israeli sages, parts of which can be traced to the time of Ezra and Nehemiah.[53] The *G'mara*, the commentary on the *Mishnah*, forms the second part of the Talmud. It is this that distinguishes the Babylonia Talmud from its lesser-known companion, the Jerusalem Talmud; the version of the Gemara in one differs from that in the other. However, the two versions are very similar. The title, the Babylonian Talmud, undoubtedly gave rise to the misinformed assumption that "Rabbinic" Judaism is a Babylonian religion. Further, as the history of the Talmud indicates, much of the material in the Talmud goes back to, or reflects, the very earliest stages of Second Temple Judaism in Israel, some of it going as far back as Ezra and his followers, as noted previously.

This means that much of Talmud predates Yeshua, parallels his teaching, and was respected by Yeshua (Matt. 23:2–3), as demonstrated previously. Therefore, most of the Talmud cannot be an attack on Yeshua and Messianic Judaism; it is too early. And the bulk of the later material is not an attack either. A two-fold motivation drives it. The first motivation seeks to understand, interpret and apply Scripture, written 500–1500 years prior, to the then "modern" situation, as Pirkey 'Avot (the section of the Talmud entitled, "The Sayings of the Fathers") clearly indicates. The second seeks to respond to the destruction of the Temple and preserve Judaism despite this great loss, as reflected in the work of the center at Yavneh. Messianic Jews inflate their own importance when they claim that the Talmud and early "Rabbinic" Judaism concerned itself primarily with attacking Messianic Judaism.

Some critics fault "the Rabbis" for Greek, not Babylonian influence. They charge "the Rabbis" with a Greek philosophical speculation and sophistry that pervert and distort God's revelation. However, they misinterpret "the Rabbis," who merely use all possible resources to understand and explain the Scriptures, which are so important to them.[54] And so, teachers such as Hillel and

Ishmael developed *middot*, or guidelines for properly interpreting Scripture, some of which may *appear* Hellenistic. As many have demonstrated, "Rabbinic" Judaism stands opposed to the Hellenistic philosophical approach.[55] So, for example, we learn that there ". . . are marked differences . . . between Hellenistic and rabbinic intellectual styles."[56] And further, as Harry Wolfson, in his edition of the works of Philo, has pointed out, there isn't a single philosophical term throughout the vast realm of rabbinic material, in other words, these are not present in Greek form or in an Aramaic or Hebrew translation of Greek philosophical terms.[57] This should surprise no one. The Pharisees, the "ancestors" of "the Rabbis," were at the forefront of the opposition to the Hellenizing of Israel during the Maccabean revolt and thereafter. And they continued to vigorously oppose the Sadducees, who were Hellenistically-inclined, throughout the Second Temple period.

Just as in interpreting Scripture, so also in understanding the traditions and reading "the Rabbis," there are essential principles to follow. It is not just content but also context, specifically including culture, which determines what is said and meant. It is not just the language of the works which must be analyzed, but also the outlook of the authors which must be taken into account. This involves a basic understanding of the differences between Semitic and Hellenistic world views and thought patterns, and an appreciation for how the rabbinic mind functions within the Semitic mindset. It is totally inadequate and highly inaccurate to interpret "the Rabbis" through the "eyes" of modernity or the "glasses" of the Western world and the "lenses" of philosophy and philology.

In dealing with the traditions, and in incorporating them, other principles must also be remembered. The focus of Messianic Judaism must remain squarely on Yeshua, and this does not mean setting aside the traditions. Further, the traditions are not authoritative, as is only the Bible. Nor are we under "the authority"[58] of the "Rabbis"; we are under Yeshua's authority! However, the prayers and teachings of "the Rabbis" are valid and helpful as they reflect and do not contradict Scripture. In fact, rather than obstacles, the traditions serve as rich and meaningful pointers to, and reinforcers of, Yeshua![59] And God used these very traditions to preserve our people through the centuries. "The Rabbis" and the traditions are not without their flaws and shortcomings, but they possess a depth, beauty and richness that are too often ignored.

Therefore, "Rabbi-bashing" should stop. We must not merely dismiss them out of hand; we can learn from them. We say we are proud of our Jewish heritage and want to preserve it, yet we continually castigate "the Rabbis," who form the basis of that heritage! Doing this is shooting ourselves in the foot. We need to grow up and take the many good things "the Rabbis" offer, rather than leave the very presumptuous impression that we are the only good Jewish people.

1. S. Ackerman, "Rabbinic Lore Vindicated by Prayers from the Past," *Jerusalem Post*, October 27, 1990; L. Schiffman, "The Dead Sea Scrolls and the Early History of Jewish Liturgy," in L. Levine, *The Synagogue In Late Antiquity* (New York: Jewish Theological Seminary, 1987).

2. See P. Carrington, *The Primitive Christian Calendar: A Study In the Making of the Marcan Gospel* (Cambridge: University Press, 1952); M. Goulder, *Midrash and Lection in Matthew* (London: SPCK, 1974); M. Goulder, *The Evangelist Calendar: A Lectionary Explanation of the Development of Scripture* (London: SPCK, 1978); and A. Guilding, *The Fourth Gospel and Jewish Worship* (Oxford: Clarendon Press, 1960).

3. Cf J. Isaac, *Jesus and Israel* (New York: Holt, Rinehart, Winston, 1971), on these and other similar parallels. It should be noted that there is ample evidence that the 'Amidah and other parts of the liturgy predate Yeshua. See, e.g., A.Z. Idelsoh, *Jewish Liturgy*; J.H. Hertz, *The Authorized Daily Prayer Book*; L. Schiffman, "The Dead Sea Scrolls."

4. For these terms, see Bauer, Arndt, Gingrich, *A Greek-English Lexicon of the New Testament* (Chicago: Univ. Of Chicago Press, 1967).

5. See, e.g., the discussion in D. Daube, *The New Testament and Rabbinic Judaism* (London: Univ. of London Press, 1956), pp. 55f; P. Lapide, *The Sermon On The Mount* (Maryknoll, NY: Orbis Books, 1986), pp. 41f.

6. "Preview: The Jerusalem Synoptic Commentary," *The Jerusalem Perspective*, March 1988, p 4.

7. See the discussion in E. Schurer, *The History Of the Jewish People in the Age of Jesus Christ*, revised by G. Vermes, et al. (Edinburgh: T. & T. Clark, 1979), vol. II, p. 433f.; R. Blizzard, "Inspiration and the Oral Law," *Yavo Digest*, vol. 2, no. 3. 1988, pp. 1f. Also see the citations in notes 13 & 16.

8. L. Schiffman, "The Significance of the Dead Sea Scrolls," *Bible Review*, October 1990, p.25.

9. B. Gerhardsson, *Memory and Manuscript* (Gleerup: Lund, 1961).

10. Cf. D. Bivin, "Jesus' Education," *Jerusalem Perspective*, vol. 2., nos. 2–3, November 1988 & December 1988; S. Safrai & M. Stern, eds., *The Jewish People In The First Century*, vol 2 (Assen: Van Gorcum, 1976).

11. W. Ong, *Orality and Literacy* (London: Routledge, 1988).

12. W.F. Albright & C.S. Mann, *Matthew*, The Anchor Bible, vol. 26 (New York: Doubleday, 1987), p. clxvi.

13. See, e.g., Lapide, *Sermon*; G. Friedlander, *The Jewish Sources of the Sermon on*

the Mount (KTAV, 1911); C.G Montefiore, *Rabbinic Literature and Gospel Teachings* (KTAV, 1970).

14. See J. Klausner's discussion, *Jesus of Nazareth* (London: George Allen and Unwin, Ltd., 1925), pp. 122, 278.

15. See D. Flusser's discussion, *Jesus* (New York: Herder and Herder, 1969), pp. 48f.

16. On this, cf. S.T. Lachs, *A Rabbinic Commentary on the New Testament* (Hoboken, NJ: KTAV, 1987).

17. See D. Flusser, "Son of Man," *The Crucible of Christianity*, ed. A. Toynbee (London: Thomas and Hudson, 1969), p. 224; H. Alford, *The Greek Testament*, vol. 1 (Chicago: Moody Press, 1968), pp. 359–360; or G.M. Lamsa's translation, *The New Testament According To The Eastern Texts*.

18. S. Safrai, "Religion in Everyday Life," in S. Safrai and M. Stern, eds., *The Jewish People In The First Century*, vol II (Philadelphia: Fortress Press, 1976).

19. Cf, e.g., A. Finkel, *The Pharisees and the Teacher of Nazareth* (Leiden: E.J. Brill, 1964); W. Phipps, "Jesus the Prophetic Pharisee," *Journal of Ecumenical Studies*, 1977; H. Falk, *Jesus the Pharisee* (New York: Paulest Press, 1985).

20. *The Jewish Reclamation Of Jesus* (Grand Rapids: Zondervan, 1984), pp. 171–190.

21. For further development of this, see R. Brooks. *The Spirit Of The Ten Commandments: Shattering The Myth Of Rabbinic Legalism* (San Francisco: Harper and Row, 1990); S. Riskin, "The Spirit of the Law Is As Important As the Letter," *Jerusalem Post*, Aug. 18, 1990.

22. In H. Kung, *Signposts For The Future* (New York: Doubleday and Co., 1978), pp. 74–75.

23. *Jesus of Nazareth*, p. 216.

24. Cf. the discussion by H.L. Ellison, "Paul and the Law," *Apostolic History and The Gospel*, eds. F.F. Bruce. W.W. Gasque, R.P. Martin (Grand Rapids: Eerdmans Publishing Co., 1970).

25. For a more complete discussion of these issues, see J. Fischer, "Paul in His Jewish Context," *Evangelical Quarterly*, July 1985, pp. 211–256.

26. For a more complete discussion of Galatians in this respect, see the series of articles "Messianic Midrash," by J. Fischer, in *The Messianic Outreach*, from Autumn 1988 through Summer 1989.

27. *The Jewish-Christian Argument* (New York: Rinehart and Winston, 1968), p. 42.

28. *Epistle of Paul To The Galatians* (Grand Rapids: Eerdmans Publishing Co., 1965), p. 12.

29. "Paul and the Law," p. 199

30. Hegessipus, a second-century church historian and leader, quoted in Eusebius, *Ecclesiastical History* (Grand Rapids: Baker Book House, 1969), pp. 75–79.

31. J. Jocz, *The Jewish People And Jesus Christ* (London: SPCK, 1962), pp. 201, 383 note 1.

32. Cf. the discussion in A Z. Idelsohn, *Jewish Liturgy* (New York: Schocken Books, 1975), pp. 104–105; my argument is based on a presentation by Rabbi M. Gruber in the course "Liturgy of the Jewish People," Spertus College of

Judaica, Fall 1976, in which Gruber also pointed out that the evidence for a late, rather than early, date for the fifteenth benediction is now considered very strong. M. Wilson, in *Our Father Abraham* (Eerdmans), pp. 65–69, also concludes that the *minim* blessing was not composed or directed against the early Messianic movement. Although some parts of the movement, specifically the Ebionites, strayed from biblical positions, other parts, such as the Nazarenes, did not. See, e.g., F. Bagatti, *The Church From The Circumcision* (Jerusalem: Franciscan Press, 1971); R. Pritz, *Nazarene Jewish Christianity* (Jerusalem: Magnes Press, 1988); J. Danielou, *The Theology of Jewish Christianity* (Chicago: Regnery, 1964).

33. *Biblical Archaeologist*, June 1988, p 70.
34. G. Vermes, *Post-Biblical Jewish Studies* (Leiden: E.J. Brill, 1975), p. 175. I. Abrahams, "By the (Expressed) Name," in G. Alon, *Jews, Judaism and the Classical World* (Jerusalem: Magnes Press, 1977), pp. 235–251, suggests that the *minim* were the Sadducees. Vermes (pp. 169–177) concludes that the *minim* came from within Hellenistic Judaism, perhaps having some gnostic leanings. Also see R. Kimelman, "*Birkat Haminim* and the Lack of Evidence for an Anti-Christian Jewish Prayer in Late Antiquity," *Jewish and Christian Self-Definition*, Vol. 2, edited by E.P. Sanders (Philadelphia: Fortress Press, 1981), pp. 226–244, 391–403.
35. *Judaism* (Baltimore: Penguin Books, 1975), p. 107
36. During the *tashlikh* ceremony the family gathers by a body of water and throws either bread or stones into the water. As the objects sink out of sight, the family recites Mic. 7:18–20.
37. See the Rosh HaShanah service in J. Fischer, ed., *Messianic Services for Festivals and Holy Days* (Palm Harbor, FL: Menorah Ministries, 1992)
38. The swinging of the chicken over the heads of the participants with the accompanying request that the chicken's death serve as a basis for "entering into a long and happy life."
39. For more on these traditions. and on the significance of the holidays, see J. Fischer, *The Meaning and Importance Of The Jewish Holidays* (Palm Harbor, FL: Menorah Ministries, 1979).
40. J. Fischer and D. Bronstein, eds., *Siddur For Messianic Jews* (Palm Harbor, FL: Menorah Ministries, 1988), p. 119.
41. Fischer and Bronstein, *Siddur*, p. 155.
42. C.G. Montefiore & H. Loewe, *Rabbinic Anthology* (New York: Schocken Books, 1974), p. 88.
43. *Paul: Rabbi and Apostle* (Minneapolis: Augsburg, 1984), p. 39.
44. "Law, Grace, Faith, and Works," in *Yavo Digest*, vol 2. no. 3, 1988, p. 4.
45. Found in *Explorations*, vol. 3, no. 1, 1989, p. 1. Similar strong positions on this issue are taken and described by Brooks, *Spirit*; Riskin, "Spirit"; and S. Schechter, *Aspects Of Rabbinic Theology* (New York: Schocken, 1972).
46. *The Rabbinic Mind* (New York: Bloch Publishing Co., 1972), p. 318. It should further be noted that in no way did "the Rabbis" seek to exclude the concept of sacrifice from Judaism. The hope for the restoration of the sacrifice system was expressed continually in the daily (fifth benediction), Sabbath and festival *'Amidah* (seventeenth benediction). In fact, the biblical passages pre-

scribing the specific holiday sacrifices are recited as part of each festival *musaf* service.

47. J H. Charlesworth, ed., *The Old Testament Pseudepigrapha* (Garden City, NY: Doubleday and Co., 1985), vol 2, pp. 634–635.

48. M. Wyschogrod in M. Tannenbaum, M. Wilson, J. Rudin, eds., *Evangelicals and Jews In Conversation* (Grand Rapids: Baker Book House, 1978), p. 39.

49. H.L. Donin, *To Be A Jew* (New York: Basic Books, 1972), pp. 11–12. See also S. Shechter's discussion in *Aspects Of Rabbinic Theology* (New York: Schocken Books, 1961), pp. 58–62.

50. A.W. Miller, "The Limits of Change in Judaism: Reshaping Prayer," *Conservative Judaism*, 1986, pp. 21–28.

51. See Fischer and Bronstein, *Siddur*, pp. 180ff.

52. See J. Fischer, "Covenant, Fulfilment and Judaism in Hebrews," in this work.

53. Cf., e.g., among others, A. Steinsaltz, *The Essential Talmud* (New York: Bantam Books, 1977), pp. 3–39.

54. Cf. S. Cohen, *From The Maccabees To The Mishnah* (Philadelphia: Westminster Press, 1987), pp. 216ff.

55. These include, among others: T. Boman, *Hebrew Thought Versus Greek* (New York: W. W. Norton, 1960); E.J. Bickerman, *The Jews In The Greek Age* (Cambridge, MA: Harvard Univ. Press, 1988); S. Cohen, *From The Maccabees To The Mishnah* (Philadelphia: Westminster Press, 1987); L. Schiffman, *From Text to Tradition* (Hoboken, KTAV, 1991); S. Safrai and M. Stern, eds., *The Jewish People In The First Century*, 2 vols. (Philadelphia: Fortress Press, 1974); E. P. Sanders, *Paul and Palestinian Judaism* (Philadelphia: Fortress Press, 1977); M. Kadushin, *Organic Thinking: A Study In Rabbinic Thought* (New York: Bloch Publishing Co , 1938); I. Epstein, *Judaism* (Baltimore: Penguin Books, 1975); J.J. Collins, *Between Athens and Jerusalem* (New York: Crossroad, 1986).

56. Quoted in J. Faur, "Reading Jewish Texts With Greek Eyes," *SH'MA*, Nov 27, 1987, p. 12.

57. PHILO, Vol. 1, p. 92.

58. This concept of "the authority of the Rabbis" is frequently a badly distorted perspective and a poorly understood concept some believers share, often due to the influence of the western world Protestant and Catholic views of authority.

59. See, e.g., Fischer and Bronstein, *Siddur*, pp. 180Ff.

MODERN-DAY GODFEARERS:
A Biblical Model For Gentile Participation in Messianic Congregations

Patrice Fischer

The scene: A meeting in Jerusalem.

The time: c. 50 C.E.

The participants: The *zakeynim* and *sh'lichim* (elders and apostles).

The problem: "What are we going to do with these Gentiles who claim to be followers of Yeshua M'shicheynu—Yeshua, our Jewish Messiah?

The solution: "We should not make it difficult for the Gentiles who are turning to God" (Acts 15:19–21).

James then proceeds to mention "4 abstentions" for these Gentiles: 1) Don't eat food polluted by idols; 2) Don't engage in sexual immorality; 3) Don't eat the meat of strangled animals; 4) Don't eat blood. To twentieth-century Western people this list seems pretty simple—the only abstention those in our society have to worry about is #2—sexual immorality. Does that mean, then, that it's clear sailing for the Gentiles?

It's not quite that easy and clear. There may be more to understanding what James is telling this meeting in Jerusalem. More information is assumed as "given" in this situation that is not normally understood today.

The historical situation in Acts 15 must be uncovered in order to understand the impact and importance of these four stipulations for Gentile believers in the first century, so we can then apply that understanding of biblical truth to today's circumstances. Add to this process the tragic observation that the vast majority of today's Gentile congregations totally ignore even these four simple instructions and it becomes clear that this decision from long ago has been blatantly misunderstood and/or ignored for the past 20 centuries. If today's Messianic people want to uncover its significance, it will be a difficult (but not unfruitful) task.

The Historical Situation in Acts

It is important to understand who these Gentile believers were that were being spoken of by James. The overwhelming majority, if not all, of these Gentiles wanted to be accepted as full participants in this Jewish faith in the Jewish Messiah. They were in a special category of Gentiles called "Godfearers." Let's answer these questions: 1) Who are Godfearers? 2) What was their belief and practice? 3) How did they fit into the theological and historical scheme of the time?

1) Who were the Godfearers? "Godfearers" in the technical sense used by both Luke and Josephus refers to that special group of Gentiles who worshipped in synagogues and adopted a Jewish belief system and a Jewish lifestyle for themselves, stopping just short of formal conversion[1] (called proselytism). The Greek word that means "Godfearer" is based on a parallel term for worshippers of pagan deities. Implicit in the term are the concepts that these people claim to worship the only true God, and that they worship him with specific acts, not just with their "mental attitude."[2] Schurer defines this group by a different compound, but with the same root, which was a formal group attached to the Jewish community, distinguished both from Jews and from full proselytes.[3] According to Schurer, John 12:20 probably reflects this group in describing "Greeks who went up to worship [at the Temple] at Festival [Passover] time."

2) What was their belief and practice? It is important to realize that these Gentile Godfearers were integral parts of synagogues within Israel and throughout the Diaspora. And as noted above, they worshipped God with specific Jewish acts, not just mental assent. Not only did these acts include the 7-part Noachide commandments (see discussion later), but the Godfearers also observed the Sabbath and dietary laws, as seen in Second Temple Judaism (Judaism during the era 100 B.C.E.–70 C.E.) as the bedrock of Jewish observance.[4] Any other Jewish observances beyond these would have been a matter of personal choice. They were encouraged by Jewish teachers within the synagogue structure, and according to G.F. Moore, "it was not uncommon for the next generation [their children] to be circumcised."[5]

Cornelius, the Godfearer mentioned in Acts 10, was a Centurian at Caesarea and serves as a good example of what a Godfearer did religiously. First, he and his household were devout and Godfearing, a double adjective referring to him and his family which shows their exemplary lives characterized by Jewish norms and values. Luke also notes he gave alms liberally to people in need (which the rabbis call *tzedekah*)[6] and prayed constantly to God. These would be actions even beyond the call of "Jewish duty," even more than the minimum for Jews. Interestingly enough, one afternoon during his regular 3 o'clock prayer time (the "ninth hour," a prescribed Temple prayer time which survives in synagogue practice today—the hour evening incense was offered)[7] an angel came to Cornelius in Caesarea (a totally Gentile-built and Gentile-run city), to tell him that his prayers and his alms "had gone up for a memorial" before God. That means that they had been accepted by God in the same way that the incense at the Temple and the smoke of a burnt offering "went up" and were accepted by God. The same Greek word is used to translate in the Septuagint the Hebrew word for offering—*olah*—literally, "an ascending."[8] Then the angel instructed Cornelius to get in touch with Peter, who was in Jaffa, and the rest, as they say, is history. But note that what Cornelius did to deserve the commendation were Jewish religious acts (not just any old good deeds) and that they were accepted by the Jewish God using Jewish terminology and concepts even though Cornelius was "technically" a gentile. And there was more than just this one man—there was a whole group of Godfearers at that time all around the Roman world who totally identified themselves with the Jewish community, except for circumcision—the final step in commitment as a Jewish proselyte.

> Many Gentiles, while not prepared to enter this Jewish community as full proselytes, were attracted by the simple monotheism of Jewish synagogue worship and by the ethical standard of the Jewish way of life. . . . We may say indeed that he [Cornelius] had every qualification short of circumcision which could satisfy Jewish requirements . . . It was such Godfearers who formed the nucleus of the Christian community in one city after another.[9]

(3) How did Godfearers fit into the historical/theological scheme of the world at that time? Obviously, as we have seen, Godfearers were more than "pagans" or "foreigners" but less than proselytes. Let's examine now these differing communities of people and their status in the eyes of the Jewish community during Second Temple times.

Classes of Gentiles: Proselytes, Godfearers and Foreigners

Underlying the world view of the Greco-Roman culture at the time was an unsympathetic attitude towards Jews. In Greek and Roman literature the judgments about Jews were in general very derogatory.[10] Seen in its most militant state, during Seleucid rule, Greek culture felt that Judaism was extremely old-fashioned and too highly nationalistic to fit in with the concept of the modern Greek world. Roman culture, beginning in 70 B.C.E. in Israel under Pompey, tolerated Jewish belief as long as it allowed for Rome to have the final governmental power. Rome tended to want to keep peace in its provinces and allowed different groups under its rule to have their own religious and cultural differences. Jewishness, to Rome, was a "quaint," unattractive religion which served well to keep the Jewish nation "unified" and serving Roman interests.[11]

Passages from writers of the time—Josephus, Juvenal, and Tertullian—give us the impression that the Greco-Roman culture saw Judaism as quite ridiculous.[12] Becoming a Godfearing person was not a popular action designed to move a person to a more influential sphere—it would have the opposite effect.

Living within Israel itself at the time were Godfearers, exemplified by Cornelius and presumably also the Centurion in Luke 7 and Matt. 10, but making proselytes in an active "missionary" way was not common within Israel.

> As a rule, proselytes and Godfearers were welcomed by the Jews and regarded very highly, but there was in Palestine no active propaganda to further the cause of proselytism.[13]

However, proselytism and Godfearers were very active in the Diaspora—the Jewish communities outside of Israel. According to

Josephus, in Antioch and Syria large numbers of Gentiles attended Jewish services. "In Damascus almost the whole female part of the population was devoted to Judaism and it was quite often women of higher social standing who followed this trend.[14] (For biblical corroboration, see Acts 16:14; esp. Lydia, Acts 17:4.) Evidently these Jewish communities encouraged and welcomed Gentile proselytes and Godfearers.

> Hellenistic Judaism . . . developed an offensive against paganism . . . They were eager to show up the immorality and senselessness of idolatry and display the rationality and sublimity of Jewish monotheism. Hellenistic Judaism had an apologetic ideology . . . There were many Godfearers who accepted the one God of the Jews, but not all the law. Hellenistic Judaism had almost succeeded in making Judaism a world religion in the literal sense of the words. Early Christianity then won the victory over paganism using Jewish weapons.[15]

This knowledge of history sheds much light on James' closing remarks to the *zakeynim* and *sh'lichim* in Acts 15:21: "For Moses [the Torah] has been preached in every city [in the Diaspora] from the earliest times [since 722 B.C.E., over 700 years] and is read in the synagogues on every Sabbath." In other words, these Godfearing Gentiles who want to become full-fledged believers have already received Moses' instructions concerning how we Jews understand people are to live (the Noachide and Sinaitic covenants) through attending synagogues in their own cities. We are here recommending these four further instructions for you Gentiles who want to be Messianists, to make sure that there is no question as to what the "bottom line" of observance is by Godfearing Gentiles: the Noachide commandments, the Sabbath and dietary laws, and these four requirements.

Exactly what was expected of Gentiles by the Jewish community at this time, and what was not expected? The Jewish religious concepts of the Second Temple period held that the other nations of the world which did not follow the one true God were *goyim*—godless (at least without the true God) and/or pagan. However, for purposes of God's judgment of other nations (including his right to judge them), the Sinaitic covenant did not apply to these "goyim," having been given exclusively to Israel. Instead, the rabbis felt, as seems clear from the passage in Gen. 9:1–18, there is a covenant for all the children of Noah (i.e., the whole world), including not only people but all living creatures (see v. 10). Based on this section of Scripture, the rabbis found seven major requirements incumbent on all nations: 1) no idolatry; 2) no incest/adultery; 3) no murder; 4) no blasphemy (profanation of the name of God); 5) no theft; 6) justice towards others (see Gen. 9:5); 7) no eating flesh with blood in it and/or cutting off flesh from a living animal.[16]

To these generally-agreed-upon tenets some rabbis added others such as taking blood from a living animal. Several also mention prohibitions against witchcraft and other spiritual sorcery, such as found in Deut. 18:10–11.[17]

These then are the major categories by which God would judge all nations. To the rabbis it was clear that although God loved all his creatures and his creation, the goyim had turned away from him and would not even follow the Noachide commandments. "Again if the children of Noah could not abide [i.e., observe] the seven commandments which were enjoined upon them, how much less could they have accepted and fulfilled all the commandments of the [Sinaitic] law?"[18]

The identifying terms used by the rabbis at this time for these goyim include: the idolaters, the wicked, the enemies of Israel, the enemies of God, and others. There was a different category, however, for those goyim who did abide by the Noachide covenant. They were called "foreigners" or "aliens." Any Gentile who lived in/among Israel was enjoined, at the very least, to keep the Noachide covenant. This was their "bottom line"—if they did not, they were to be expelled. If they did keep it, they were no longer called goyim, but *gerim*. The Talmud delineates them further by the new term *ger toshev*. These were foreigners living in the land of Israel who were keeping the seven Noachide commandments.[19] By the time of the Septuagint (about 200 B.C.E.) the translators used the term "fearers" for the righteous outside of natural Israel in contrast to the term "proselytes," those righteous Gentiles who formally identified with Israel through conversion.[20]

What was the next step for these *gerim* who wanted to become "full" Jews? The first *gerim* are mentioned in the Exodus narrative. Among the Jews who left Egypt there were Egyptians who also left their homes in Egypt and crossed the Red Sea, becoming part of the people of Israel (Exod. 12:38). Although they were known as aliens—*gerim* (simply meaning that they were not physical descendants of Jacob), they could be circumcised, and thus formally convert to this very early form of Judaism, then partake of the Passover meal with the rest of Israel (at this point, Passover was the only Jewish festival). Note the differentiation between "foreigner" in Exod. 12:43 and the "alien who lives among you." The foreigner may *not* eat Passover (he is not circumcised and therefore not Jewish—see Exod. 12:48c), but the alien who is circumcised along with his household (i.e., they have converted to Judaism, become proselytes) *may* eat Passover. Verse 49 indicates that the proselyte was to have the same rights and privileges as the native-born Jew: "The same law applies to the native-born and alien." According to Exod. 12:19, the community of Israel is made up of aliens (converts/proselytes) and native-born. Consequently, these *gerim toshevim* who wanted to fully convert always could do so by becoming circumcised and then continuing to follow the Jewish way of life, which then adopted the covenant at Mt. Sinai (Exod. 24). Note also that Sabbath observance was technically commanded *before* the acceptance of the Sinaitic code (see Exod. 20:10 and 23:12). Then, although they were recognized by outward appearances as aliens, they were now Jews—they had left behind their old country and family in order to be part of the Jewish community, who had adopted them as their own. The rabbis' term for these proselytes was *gerey hatzedek*—righteous foreigners. How may proselytes there were down through the centuries is impossible to determine,[21] but the rabbis are clear about the proselytes' relationship to the rest of Israel: "A proselyte is like a newborn child."[22] The proselyte is, however, required and expected to be as strictly observant as the native-born Jew, including paying the Temple tax.[23] The book of Ruth portrays the most beautiful example of how God can highly honor a proselyte, by choosing her as the great-grandmother of David.

After the building of the Second Temple there was a recognized procedure for proselytes. For men, there was circumcision, followed by immersion (*mikveh*), then offering a sacrifice at the Temple. For women there was just the *mikveh* and Temple sacrifice. For Diaspora proselytes the Temple sacrifice was probably waived, or at least postponed.[24]

As previously noted, the Godfearers' observance of the law was located between the full proselytes and the *gerim toshev*. They were known as *gerey hasha'ir*—"foreigners of the gate."[25] To their observance of the Noachide covenant they added formal conversion, like Cornelius. The reasons for their not formally joining Judaism are not clear to us today. Some scholars, like Bruce, maintain that circumcision was both painful and shameful for men in that culture.[26] Some also might have been fearful of anti-Semitism.[27] At any rate, we do know that these Godfearers were every bit as Jewishly observant as their Jewish friends, and that they had been undergoing discipling and instruction in their local synagogues. These people were not just well-intentioned "Gentiles-on-the-street," but Jewishly educated and committed to the Jewish way of life. They, like our example Cornelius, probably were more deeply devoted to Judaism than many native-born Jews.

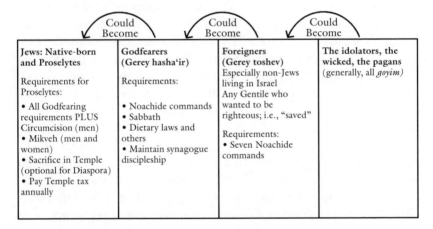

	Could Become →	Could Become →	Could Become →	
Jews: Native-born and Proselytes	Godfearers (Gerey hasha'ir)	Foreigners (Gerey toshev) Especially non-Jews living in Israel Any Gentile who wanted to be righteous; i.e., "saved"	The idolators, the wicked, the pagans (generally, all *goyim*)
Requirements for Proselytes:	Requirements:		
• All Godfearing requirements PLUS Circumcision (men) • Mikveh (men and women) • Sacrifice in Temple (optional for Diaspora) • Pay Temple tax annually	• Noachide commands • Sabbath • Dietary laws and others • Maintain synagogue discipleship	Requirements: • Seven Noachide commands	

What does this explain about Acts 15? The vision related to Peter in Acts 10 and his subsequent experience with Cornelius and his household proved to Peter (and also later to the *zakeynim* and *sh'lichim*) that it was *not necessary* for these *gerim* to proceed with full conversion to Judaism in order to receive God's provision of atonement through the Jewish Messiah. They could come as they were—Godfearing Gentiles. There were only four further abstentions they needed to be clear about (which actually delineate more clearly their already fully Jewish commitment). First, they should not eat food sacrificed to idols—this gives the appearance that they have not yet given up idolatrous practices. (Notice Rav Sha'ul and Yochanan *HaShaliach* also object to eating food sacrificed to idols in 1 Cor. 8; 10:18–22; and Rev. 2 because of the outward meaning of the action to highly observant Jews and "weaker brothers" from pagan backgrounds.) Second, they should not engage in sexual immorality—as defined by Jewish standards, which prohibit sex outside of marriage. Here again, the average "pagan Gentile" would see nothing wrong in visiting the prostitutes dedicated to serving and worshipping pagan gods—it would not be defined as immoral behavior by their standards. But it is a very grievous sin to the followers of the God of Israel (see also 1 Cor. 6:9–20), and should also be to those Godfearers who wish to follow him. Abstention from meat of strangled animals (i.e., animals killed with the blood still left in the body) and from eating blood in general are stronger reiterations of the Noachide regulations already understood and practiced by Godfearers (Gen. 9:4). James even concedes that they probably already knew these abstentions—"For Moses [the Torah] has been preached in every city. . ." These tenets would be nothing new for Godfearers.

Were circumcision and formal entry into Judaism mandatory for Godfearers who believed in Messiah? No. These former Gentile pagans who were now known as Godfearers were already practicing the Torah in their everyday lives. Israel's God accepted Cornelius and his household just as they were. He would also accept the other Godfearers as they were, provided they continued to study in the local synagogue and follow God Jewishly. By this time this included also following the four abstentions from Acts 15. But as we have seen, these abstentions were based on guidelines they were already following.

A good example of a congregation that failed even in these basic instructions was found in Corinth. It is noteworthy that Rav Sha'ul had to deal with several areas in which the group had failed to uphold the Acts 15 stipulations, including sexual immorality (one man sleeping with his father's wife, some congregants sleeping with prostitutes), and eating meat sacrificed to idols.[28] These

Corinthians were so uninformed of Jewish roots that they used the occasion of the four Passover cups at the "Lord's Supper" to get drunk! The Godfearing guidelines for the congregation had already been lost, and the people were in disarray. Their experience is a clear warning to those Gentile congregations who openly flout the Acts 15 requirements.

Summary

The Gentile Godfearers in Acts (who formed a large portion of the congregations founded by Rav Sha'ul) were not practicing pagans converted overnight. They were of a special class of Gentiles who had been taught and nurtured in their local synagogues first, worshipping the God of Israel through Jewish acts. The "bottom line" of observance for Gentiles in the Jewish world of Second Temple Judaism would have been the seven Noachide commandments. Godfearing Gentiles, however, went even further, observing the Sabbath, keeping the dietary laws (as they were understood then), plus other Jewish observances that they had been taught by their local Jewish leaders. Thus their lifestyle already identified them as Jews, even if the final ritual of formal conversion had not yet taken place. Acts 15 describes the full acceptance of these Godfearers by the leadership of Messianic Jews in Jerusalem. To what the Godfearers were already practicing, the leadership added only four additional guidelines, which were based on what the Godfearers were already practicing. If they maintained their Torah-based practices, they would have congregations and practices equal to those of their Jewish brothers and sisters. If they failed to maintain their Godfearing lifestyles and educational programs, they would fall into the traps of sin that were disrupting the Corinthian congregation.

Evaluation of the Evidence for Today's Messianic Jews

Gentiles who maintain Torah practices like biblical Godfearing Gentiles can be welcomed into full membership and leadership within Messianic congregations today. They *may* wish to formally convert to Judaism, but it is not necessary for full acceptance into God's family in general, or the Messianic synagogue in particular. As long as they maintain their active Jewish lifestyle, they can serve and lead congregations.

1. For the two Greek terms used by Luke and Josephus to describe Godfearers, see *Theological Dictionary of The New Testament*; Kittel, F., Trans. Bromley. Eerdmans: 1971. Vol. VII, pp. 169ff. Also see Kittel, Vol. VIII, pp. 202ff. esp. p. 207.

2. Kittel, Vol. VII, p. 172.

3. Schurer, Emil. *The History of the Jewish People in the Age of Jesus Christ.* Revised and edited by Vermes, Millar and Goodman. T&T Clark: 1987. Vol. III, p. 166.

4. Ibid.

5. Moore, George Foot. *Judaism in the First Centuries of the Christian Era.* Schocken: 1958. Vol. 1, p. 325.

6. The standard formula for Jewish "righteousness" since the destruction of the Temple and the cessation of sacrifice has been prayer, repentance, and *tzedekah.*

7. NIV Study Bible notes. See also Acts 3:1. Luke is very interested in giving Jewish specifics to back up his case.

8. Bruce, F.F. *Commentary on the Book of the Acts.* Eerdmans: 1970, p. 216. This phrase about his alms and prayers going up as a memorial before God is part of standard synogogue daily prayers even today.

9. Schurer, Vol. III, pp. 150–162.

10. For more information on this time period, see F.F. Bruce, *Israel and the Nations*; Edward Lohse, *The New Testament Environment*, pp. 197–252, and many others.

11. Schurer, Vol. III, pp. 166ff.

12. Juvenal's Satire, xiv, pp. 96ff.

13. Safrai, S. and Stern, M., eds. *The Jewish People in the First Century.* Fortress Press, 1976. Vol 2, p. 1095.

14. Cited in Schurer, p. 162.

15. Safrai and Stern, p. 1097.

16. See Schurer, p. 172; see also Montefiore & Loewe, *A Rabbinic Anthology.* Schocken Books: 1974. Chapter XXIX, "The Gentiles," pp. 556–565.

17. Montefiore & Loewe, p. 556.

18. Cited by Montefiore & Loewe, p. 78.

19. Schurer, p. 171.

20. Ibid.

21. Ibid.

22. Moore, vol. I, p. 334, quoting Talmudic material.

23. From Montefiore & Loewe, p. 570. For more Talmudic material, see the excellent chapter, "On Proselytes," pp. 566–579. See also Gal. 5:2 for strictness of converts.

24. Bruce, *History*, pp. 140–144.

25. Schurer, p. 171. See also Bruce, *History.*

26. Bruce, *History*, pp. 140–144.

27. Brown, Colin, ed. *Dictionary of New Testament Theology*, Vol. 1, pp. 360ff.

28. A man's sleeping with his father's wife is strictly forbidden to Israel: Lev. 18:8; Deut. 22:30; 27:20. Note that the Corinthian man is to be punished by the same punishment as an Israelite—expulsion.

CONTRIBUTORS

John Fischer, Ph.D., Th.D.—Dr. Fischer is Executive Director of Menorah Ministries, Academic Vice President for St. Petersburg Theological Seminary, *Rosh Yeshiva* (Head) of Netzer David International Yeshiva, Rabbi of Congregation Ohr Chadash, and a founder of the Union of Messianic Jewish Congregations. He serves on the Executive Committee of the International Messianic Jewish Alliance.

Patrice Fischer, D.Min.—Dr. Fischer is the Chair of the Division of Historical and Cultural Studies at St. Petersburg Theological Seminary, where she is Professor of Hebrew and Professor of Jewish Scripture. She is also on the adjunct faculty of the University of South Florida.

Louis Goldberg, Th.D.—Dr. Goldberg was for many years the chair of the Jewish Studies department of Moody Bible Institute. He has taught in Israel and is Scholar-in-Residence for Jews for Jesus.

Walter Kaiser, Ph.D.—Dr. Kaiser is the president of Gordon-Conwell Theological Seminary, where he is also the Colman M. Mockler distinguished professor of Old Testament. He is the author of numerous books and an internationally recognized scholar and speaker.

Elliot Klayman, Esq.—Mr. Klayman is a professor at Ohio State University. He was the president of the Union of Messianic Jewish Congregations and continues to serve on their Executive Committee.

Lawrence J. Rich—Mr. Rich is a former rabbi of Adat HaTikvah Messianic Congregation in Chicago and is currently the Vice President and Director of North American Ministries for Chosen People Ministries.

Michael Schiffman, D.Min.—Dr. Schiffman has served on the Executive Committee of the Union of Messianic Jewish Congregations and as the leader of Kehilat Yeshua Messianic Congregation in New York City. He is the director of Anshe Rachamim.

David Stern, Ph.D., M.Div.—Dr. Stern is the translator of the *Complete Jewish Bible* and of the *Jewish New Testament*, as well as the author of the *Jewish New Testament Commentary*. He is a long time resident of Jerusalem.